CASTE, CLASS AND DEMOCRACY:

Changes in a Stratification System

CASTE, CLASS AND DEMOCRACY:

Changes in a Stratification System

VIJAI P. SINGH

SCHENKMAN PUBLISHING COMPANY

Cambridge, Massachusetts

Library of Congress Catalog Card Number:

76-7841

Singh, Vijai

   Caste, class and democracy.

Mass.   Schenkman Publishing Co.
April 1976   3-11-76

ISBN   87073-576-4 cloth
         87073-577-2 paper

Preface

This book examines the changes in the social stratification of three Indian communities between 1930–1965. Important studies dealing with different aspects of stratification carried out in various parts of India are reviewed, to provide some continuity with previous research on the one hand and to present a broader picture of stratification on the other.

The nature of stratification is studied by investigating the degree of association among the relevant stratification dimensions. The changes in the degree of such associations and mobility on various dimensions across time demonstrate the changing patterns of the status system. During three and one-half decades the amount of inequalities in both caste status and political power declined. Intergenerational mobility in both education and occupation increased, but concomitantly, the reduced inequalities became at once more ordered and also more rigid with respect to the constraints of caste. It was noted, for instance, that sons with higher caste background were more likely to acquire higher educational and occupational status than others. During the later period, higher caste persons used their resources generously and encouraged their sons to aspire for higher education and prestigious jobs. Thus, the ascriptive advantages were used to acquire superior status in areas essentially based on achievement. For the same reason, and despite important institutional and legislative changes at the village level, lower caste persons experienced but limited success in improving their position in the stratification system. Their future now would seem to depend mainly upon employment opportunities outside agriculture and an anonymous urban environment where they can free themselves from traditional relations.

I would like to acknowledge my gratitude towards several organizations and individuals for their help and encouragement. A fellowship from the National Institute of Community Development, Hyderabad, (previously at Mussoorie), India enabled me to prepare the research design and collect the data for this study. I am most grateful to my respondents for their time and patience. The University of Wisconsin Research Committee and The Department of Sociology, Cornell University financed the computer time. Small grants from the Faculty Grants Committee and Asian Studies program at the University of Pittsburgh helped meet some of the research expenses. A N.I.H. Post-doctoral Fellowship during 1970–71 enabled me to devote some of my time in the preparation of this monograph, which originally was presented in 1970 (in a different version) as a Ph.D Thesis at the University of Wisconsin.

Professors Joseph W. Elder, Archibald O. Haller, H. Kent Geiger and William H. Sewell at the University of Wisconsin, Madison were constant sources of intellectual stimulation and helped me in various ways in the preparation of my dissertation. I am grateful for their patience and understanding during critical times. The criticisms of Professors Gerhard Lenski, Leonard Reissman and Harold Gould were very helpful and I am thankful to them. Among my colleagues, Rainer Baum and Norman Hummon read the manuscript, and their comments and criticisms proved valuable. I am thankful to them.

Professor Thomas Lasswell, editor of The Stratification Series in which this monograph is published, read the manuscript and made valuable suggestions for its reorganization. Mrs. Eva Greenberg of The Social Systems Training Program, Department of Sociology, Cornell University helped in data analysis and preparation of tables. Their help is most appreciated.

Vijai P. Singh

Pittsburgh, Pa.

Contents

Preface   v

Contents   vii

PART I

THE CONCEPTS AND THEORIES OF SOCIAL STRATIFICATION

Introduction	3
Marx and Weber	4
The Contemporary Functionalists	7
The Synthesis	10
The Concept of Social Stratification	11
The Concept of Social Mobility	12
The Concept of Social Class	14

PART II

CONCEPTUALIZATION OF SOCIAL STRATIFICATION IN INDIA

Caste Stratification	21
Mobility in the Caste System	23
Caste and Occupation	25
The Dimensions of Stratification	27
The External Forces	29
Caste and Class	31
Recent Institutional Changes	35
Changes in Three Indian Villages	38
The Unit of Analysis	40
The Data	46

PART III

THE STRATIFICATION VARIABLES

Caste Status	51
Property Status	59
Political Power	63
Educational Status	66
Occupational Status	68

PART IV

CHANGES IN THE STRATIFICATION SYSTEM

Caste Inequality   75
Changes in Caste Inequality   77
Economic and Political Inequality   80
Changes in Economic Status and Power   82
Educational and Occupational Inequality   87
Changes in Educational and Occupational Inequality   87
The Intergenerational Analysis   90
The Stratification System and Intergenerational Change

                                                           97
Educational and Occupational Mobility   99
The Two Class System   108
Status Consistency   117

PART V

CONCLUSIONS AND SOME THEORETICAL APPLICATIONS

                                                           121

BIBLIOGRAPHY

                                                           136

APPENDIX A

INTERCORRELATIONS AMONG FAMILY POSSESSIONS IN THE THREE VILLAGES

                                                           145

APPENDIX B

DISTRIBUTION OF OCCUPATIONS ACROSS GENERATIONS IN THE THREE VILLAGES

                                                           146

APPENDIX C

INTERCORRELATIONS AMONG THE STRATIFICATION VARIABLES OVER THE THREE GENERATIONS

                                                           148

INDEXES

                                                           152

CASTE, CLASS AND DEMOCRACY:

Changes in a Stratification System

Part One

The Concepts and Theories of Social Stratification

INTRODUCTION

The major theoretical concern behind this research is to study the changes in a stratification system over time and to identify the important societal factors that have influenced the process. Generally, sociologists have paid much attention to the consequences of different stratification systems. Less attention has been given to internal social structural factors and radical institutional and legislative changes that may shape the profile of the stratification system. We will, therefore, examine in this volume how institutionalized inequalities are created and distributed, particularly in India.

Most of the empirical research on social stratification has been concentrated on North America and certain Western European countries. Many of the findings and implications may not be applicable to other societies. In the study of stratification, cultural and political differences between societies should be taken into consideration. Many societies are not as technologically and economically developed as the Western societies, so we may expect to find different structural conditions for stratification. In some non-Western societies internal heterogeneity is so pronounced that dual stratification may coexist.[1]

Today, many students of social stratification postulate that occupation is the most important index of social stratification in highly industrialized societies and therefore, the study of occupational structure is crucial to understanding social stratification. The implication is, of course, that occupational status signifies or is the source of differential economic status, power and prestige. It has been reported occasionally that cultural differences and differences in the level of economic development between societies do not produce similarity in the evaluation of occupations. This debate is not settled yet, and more data are needed from within such societies before a definite position can be established.[2]

3

There is some evidence which suggests that occupational status as a prestige hierarchy may not be the most important source of differences in economic or political power. Lenski has shown that in less industrialized societies, personal ability, personal characteristics, inheritance, personal relations with the political head, ethnic background, and religious affiliations are important factors which determine one's access to power and privilege. As a society develops technologically, social, economic and political institutions emerge, which are associated with the loss of significance of hereditary statuses. It is only after a society has reached a mature industrial stage that occupational status becomes a major source of power and privilege.[3] It may be stated then, that societies show a wide range of variations in their stratification systems and that our knowledge of stratification systems is based on too small a sample of societies. Serious attempts are yet to be made to examine systematically changes in stratification systems of many non-Western societies.

National leaders and planners throughout the world emphasize in their speeches and policy papers the need to improve the conditions of the masses and to reduce inequalities. Much of this concern may be political rhetoric. Knowledge about the nature and extent of institutionalized inequality can facilitate realistic programs of planned change. The basic question of our limited understanding of stratification systems needs to be answered. A comparative perspective on stratification can emerge only after more definitive studies that cover a wide spectrum of time and space have been made.

A brief review of some of the literature on stratification should be presented before discussing theoretical and methodological issues that surround this research. Theories and concepts that are of particular relevance to this research are discussed here, and of course they do not exhaust the enormous body of literature on social stratification.

MARX AND WEBER:

Karl Marx argued that a man's position in the social structure is determined by his role in the system of production. Economic and social forces create conditions in which social groups have comparable ranks on various dimensions of social stratification. These forces result in the formation of two antagonistic social classes — the bourgeoisie and the proletariat. A man's relationship to the means of production is the basis for class formation in which the bourgeois are the owners of the means of production while the proletariat own nothing more than their own labor. People who occupy similar positions in the work environment belong to similar classes. Therefore, "Free man and slave, patrician and plebeian, lord and serf, guildmaster and journeyman, in a word, oppressor and oppressed, stand in constant opposition to one another . . ."[4] This class-based stratification is found in all societies in all historical periods. The nature of class relations depends upon the ownership of property and mode of production.

Marx also mentioned three classes in his writing and it was at this point that he seemed to be engaging in the elaboration of his theory of class. He raised the question "What constitutes a class?" — and the reply to another question, namely, "what makes wage laborers, capitalists and landlords constitute the three great social classes?"[5] Dichotomous and trichotomous conceptions of class were based on the contexts in which Marx used them. The former was analytic and useful in explaining social change while the latter provided the description of society.[6]

The two-class conception of society has been a point of greater controversy in the contemporary social sciences because of the polarization and eventual revolutionary consequences which Marx envisaged. Dahrendorf pointed out that Marx's two classes originated from the ownership of the means of production and served only a heuristic purpose in social analysis. The Marxian theory of classes was more useful in the explanation of social change than of social stratification.[7]

Marx did have a multi-dimensional conception of class. He assigned the greatest importance to the economic aspect of social organization, to the extent of neglecting its power element. Power, according to Marx, is treated as a resource to achieve economic supremacy and is not a goal in itself.[8] Heller pointed out that for Marx, power was a central concept in reflecting economic and social inequality. The fact that he believed that the ownership of the means of production bestowed enormous power to rule non-owners indicated that Marx was aware of the salience of power in the stratification system.[9] Classes were real for Marx and class consciousness was necessary for their organization and effectiveness.[10] For Marx, classes were indispensable tools for understanding exploitative relations which resulted in revolutions and changes in ideological and institutional thrusts. Marx saw classes as having a profound impact on the major institutions of society and the relations between men.

Marx's theory of social stratification has been critically examined by Bendix, Lipset, Dahrendorf and Barber to mention only a few.[11] They agreed that Marx saw ownership of economic resources as pivotal in determining the nature of a stratification system. However, Marx's perspective of class was too narrow to be applicable across time and space in the explanation of stratification systems generally. Class consciousness, polarization and revolution, which the Marxian theory of class envisaged, are more ideologically validated than empirically observed in industrial societies. The potential for rebellions and revolutions is more likely to be present in underdeveloped countries which have experienced a "revolution of rising expectations," in countries where a tiny proportion of the population monopolizes economic and political power in the midst of an impoverished but increasingly hopeful majority. Despite its ideological perspective, the Marxian theory of class may be a useful tool for social analysis in the underdeveloped nations, even if not in its original form.

The concept of class as one form of social stratification is indeed relevant to most particular historical and social structural contexts; however, some theoretical inadequacies may result when Marx's theory of social class is applied narrowly. The result may be the exclusion of noneconomic stratification variables that may in fact have consequences similar to those which Marx predicted from their relations to the mode of production alone. The contemporary world has witnessed exploitation, oppression and even the breakup of nation states, not so much as a result of economic modes of production, but due to a greater extent to such noneconomic factor as religion and ethnic and racial antagonism. The specification of a single factor for the explanation of all social stratification should be made with the utmost caution no matter how frequently that factor appears to be related: what seems to be a simple explanation may actually be a distortion of emipircal reality.

Max Weber was more aware of the complexities of society than Marx. He suggested a multidimensional approach to social stratification. Weber's conceptualization of class has an economic basis, with a man's class position determined by the type of property he possesses and the kind of service he offers in the market place.[12] Weber made this point explicit when he stated that ". . . the factor that creates 'class' is unambiguously economic interest, and indeed, only those interests involved in the existence of the 'market'."[13] The propertied classes are at the top and live on the income from property; middle classes own various types of property and skills and derive their income from them, and below these two classes are non-owners of property or skills.[14] Weber, unlike Marx, cautioned that class struggle is not inevitable and in fact, classes of owners and non-owners may coexist and may even have ties of solidarity.[15] Whether people in similar class situations will organize to act collectively depends upon whether they themselves relate to the cultural context.[16]

In contrast to classes which are economically determined, status groups, according to Weber, are based upon the social estimation of honor. Although status honor may not be associated with property status, they are often linked. Status honor is based on style of life and a status group may exclude others from interaction.[17] Social status rests on (i) mode of living, (ii) formal education, (iii) prestige of birth, (iv) prestige of occupations, or prohibitions from certain modes of acquisition. Weber argued that property status and professional status are not sufficient to acquire social status but they may help when other conditions are favorable. Also, social status may determine class status, but people of diverse income and professional background may constitute a status group.[18] Weber suggested that the relationship between classes and status groups is complex and should be studied in specific contexts.

Weber labeled a status group with distinct conventions, laws and rituals as fully developed. Status groups may be open or closed; a caste is an example of a closed status group. A style of life which involves monopolization of ideals, conventions, material goods and opportunities is elaborately practiced by the upper status groups.[19] The upper castes in India rigidly practice endogamy and commensality; it is a disqualification for caste members to perform physical labor or to come in contact with objects which are polluting. The upper castes can therefore be considered to be fully developed status groups.

According to Weber, another important dimension of stratification is power. It is exercised by "parties." Party actions may be rationally planned to achieve certain goals or may be oriented to enhance prestige for their leaders and followers. The power structure is influenced by the social structure in which it is welded, and may represent elements from both classes and status groups.[20]

For Marx, greater control of economic resources guaranteed greater access to prestige and power. Objective conditions determined the attitudes and actions of individuals within the system. In contrast, Weber's conception of stratification emerged from the consideration of a multitude of subjective as well as objective aspects of social reality. The subjective evaluation in the context of status groups and objective evaluation in the context of class status and power status are related in complex ways. The specification by Weber of three distinct but related dimensions of stratification made it possible for researchers to investigate empirically these relationships across time in order to understand changes in stratification systems. It allowed for a broader scheme than one based strictly on relationships to the means of production.

THE CONTEMPORARY FUNCTIONALISTS

Contemporary social scientists have studied with great interest causes and consequences of inequality. A systematic examination of related issues was undertaken when Davis and Moore proposed their functional theory of social stratification.[21] They argued that inequality is a functional necessity in all societies. They also maintained that a society must generate the mechanisms for motivating select individuals to prepare themselves adequately to occupy positions requiring skills and talents beneficial to the functioning of the whole society. For this process to be successful, "a society must have, first, some kind of rewards that it can use as inducements, and, second, some way of distributing these rewards differentially according to positions. The rewards and their distribution become a part of the social order and thus give rise to stratification."[22] The justification of the resulting inequality is considered not only functionally necessary but universal. They argue, "social inequality is thus an unconsciously evolved device by which societies ensure that the most important positions are conscientiously filled by the most qualified persons. Hence every society, no matter how simple or complex, must differentiate persons in terms of both prestige and esteem, and must therefore possess a certain amount of institutionalized inequality."[23]

Inequality comes about by ranking positions on the basis of their functional importance and the availability of talented and trained personnel to fill them. Therefore, both higher rewards and prestige in society accrue to positions of greater functional importance which require qualified personnel.

In the functionalist tradition, Parsons suggested that stratification rests on the common value system of a society and that it is integrative in nature.[24] In one of his recent articles, he pointed out that inequality in modern society is justified on the basis of functional needs, even though there is great emphasis on the ideological doctrine that individuals be treated as equals.[25] Positional inequality based on achievement will persist while such ascriptive bases of status as race, ethnicity, caste, etc., will decline. There will be greater emphasis on equality of opportunity but Parsons declared that, "I shall here maintain my older view that the institutionalization of stratification, or more precisely of relations of inequality of status, constitutes an essential aspect in the solution of the problem of order in the social systems through the legitimation of essential inequalities; but the same holds pari passu, for the institutionalization of patterns of equality. . . . All societies institutionalize some balance between equality and inequality."[26] It was assumed that such a balance would be rationally sought, in the best interests of the society as a whole, and that it would be understood and accepted by all segments of population.

Criticisms and comments have poured forth on the functional theory of stratification; most of these were directed towards various elements of the Davis and Moore theory. The major criticism centered on the "functional importance" of a position. This concept was not spelled out in operational terms by Davis and Moore, or Parsons. Tumin maintained that in a highly stratified society, one cannot assume that all talented persons will get an equal chance of being identified.[27] He asserted that contrary to functionalist assumptions, social stratification may be devisive instead of being integrative and may fail to utilize available human and material resources. The functionalist notion of inequality favors the maintenance of a status quo as though it is logical, natural and morally right for society to be constructive.

The assumption of equality of opportunity in the Davis and Moore theory is difficult to validate empirically. Parsons has acknowledged that inequalities of opportunity exist and has suggested that people ought to make deliberate attempts to remove barriers through social action.[28] In any society, the current structure of inequality is influenced by the preceding ones and the position of each generation in the stratification system is affected by the previous generations. Therefore, ascription plays an important part in the distribution of inequalities. This fact seems to be neglected by the functionalists.[29] Porter attributed this neglect to conservatism in America when he stated that "the functional theory of stratification reflects the American conservative ideology that inequality is necessary and that people more or less arrive at the class positions which they deserve. Because of its simplicity the theory also has a popular appeal. Many of the problems arising from the structure of class in Canada . . . can be argued away by the functional theory."[30] Other critics have felt that the functional theory of stratification has not dealt adequately with the issue of legitimacy and distribution of power.[31] Although Davis and Moore have referred to power and its unequal distribution, they have not indicated how it could be integrated with other elements of the theory.

Functional theory is most applicable where achievement is the predominant basis of inequality, and accordingly it may fail to highlight ascriptive mechanisms in the distribution of inequality.[32] Davis failed to show how caste can fit in with the assumptions of functional theory.[33] He suggested that the problem of ascription can be tackled by taking the family as the unit of analysis and investigating its influence on mobility patterns.[34] He pointed out that in a closed stratification system, the status of children is completely determined by the status of their parents, while in a completely open stratification system parental status has absolutely no effect in determining the status of children. "Open" and "closed" systems are theoretical ideal types; however, in reality most stratification systems are of a mixed nature.[35] The functionalist assumption of a completely open system seems to be based more on ideology than on observation of societies generally. This issue will be discussed in detail later in the context of social mobility and classes.

A review of the functional theory of stratification and comments made by various scholars reveals that its treatment of power and ascription are peripheral at best. This, of course, limits the scope of the theory. Huaco has been most sympathetic towards functional theory but he, too, writes that "Tumin is unquestionably correct in taking power as a major determinant of role ascription, and a power explanation goes a long way in accounting for why the present incumbents of high-reward positions are who they are."[36] Therefore, either a more flexible approach should be adopted or ascription and power should be given a more convincing place in the functional theory of stratification.

THE SYNTHESIS

Both conflict and functionalist theories try to explain the mechanisms by which stratification is created and maintained. The former argues that since valued goals are scarce in society, individuals and groups use coercion to possess them and the weaker sections of society are exploited by the dominant groups. We have already seen that the exponents of functional theory suggest that social stratification is functionally necessary and therefore, a universal and permanent feature of all societies. They also maintain that stratification originates from common values and rests on consensus. The debate over the respective claims of conflict and functional theories are far from settled. Some scholars believe that the two approaches are complementary to each other. Other social scientists suggest that it is fruitless to argue the adequacy of one over the other, that instead both should be taken as differing perspectives and applied in particular contexts.

Lenski was not content with either functional or conflict theory as such. He proposed a "synthesis" theory to study inequality, using empirical data instead of logic in testing his hypotheses.[37] He pointed out that unsuccessful attempts for a synthesis have been made before, and the effort should not be abandoned because neither the "radical" (conflict) nor the "conservative" (functional) theories have explained systems of inequality adequately.[38] He claimed that much of the past effort for a synthesis "has been more by drift than by design."[39] He outlined the basic issues that divide radicals and conservatives as (i) the nature of man (ii) the nature of society (iii) maintenance of inequality and social conflict (iv) sources of rights and privileges (v) the inevitability of inequality (vi) the nature of state and law and (vii) the conception of class.[40] Lenski examined these issues in great detail and showed that sometimes empirical reality is at variance with prevalent beliefs.[41]

The major concern in Lenski's formulation is who gets what and why; this reflects a Marxian preoccupation with the distribution of goods and services.[42] He identified the social forces that generate surplus in a society and also the principles of distribution which result in inequality. This pattern of increasing inequality reaches its peak in agrarian societies, but reverses itself in advanced industrial societies. Power is central to the distributive sytsem; however, it is fluid and shows variations in its effect in different historical periods and in different technological contexts. In advanced industrial societies, for instance, social, economic and political structures become more differentiated and various occupational groups engage in bargaining which results in a more equitable distribution of society's resources.[43] Whether Lenski succeeded in his initial aim of developing a synthesis theory may still be debated by many, but his attempt has certainly provided a less rigid approach for studying stratification.

THE CONCEPT OF SOCIAL STRATIFICATION

Currently, there is a reasonable degree of agreement among social scientists regarding the definition of social stratification. Social stratification refers to the process of placing differentiated social units along an idealized continuum, or to the conceptualization of these social units into categories which share a relatively common position with respect to a socially validated scale of specific or generalized characteristics. These units may be individuals, families, classes, nations or any identifiable unit that one might conceptualize in an hierarchial order. In principle, a stratification system can be unidimensional or multidimensional. The type of system should be based upon the kind of society that is being studied and the nature of association among the elements of the stratification system. In other words, "a society characterized by perfect correlation between all relevant criterion variables has a one dimensional stratification system. Conversely, one in which the average correlation is lower will be multidimensional. Furthermore, to the extent that it can be shown that only one rank factor varies markedly in a society, whereas others are approximately constant, then again a one dimensional model will fit that case."[44] The number of dimensions and their relative salience may differ from society to society and between different historical periods.

Most contemporary writers on stratification use several dimensions of stratification; the most commonly used are the ones suggested by Max Weber. Weber identified economic status, prestige and political power as the major dimensions of stratification in his famous article on class, status and party.[45] For this study, it is assumed that stratification is multidimensional. Varying emphasis is placed on different dimensions in different times and places. Some of these dimensions are ascriptive, some are achievement-based; some involve subjective, some objective, evaluations.

The nature of stratification can be studied by investigating changes in the strength of associations among stratification dimensions.[46] An imperfect association between stratification dimensions is defined as status inconsistency. Status inconsistency has been shown to have identifiable social and psychological consequences,[47] and may exert pressure on an individual or a social system to change. Weak associations among stratification dimensions show that the major institutions of society are in a process of transition and that the stratification system is less structured and institutionalized.

THE CONCEPT OF SOCIAL MOBILITY

The concept of social mobility is involved in the understanding of the internal dynamics of a stratification system. Social mobility is defined as the movement of social units from one position to another.[48] The principal types of mobility are horizontal and vertical. In the former the transition occurs at the same level. Vertical mobility has two directions that are described by Sorokin as "ascending and descending, or social climbing and social sinking."[49] The amount and type of social mobility influences the nature of a stratification system.

The various dimensions of stratification can be conceived as locating social positions in which mobility may occur between generations. In the context of intergenerational mobility, the degree of association between the status of parents and the status of children is inversely related to the degree of mobility in the stratification system. The lower the association, the greater the mobility.

Societies may resemble one another in the profiles of their stratification systems but still differ in the degree of mobility. This would indicate the "openness" or "closedness" of the status system, which leads us into "class" and "caste" models of the stratification system. Sorokin argues that it would be difficult to claim that any society is either completely free and unhampered by social barriers or that it is completely closed.[50] It has been suggested that mobility becomes more probable during times of rapid social change and especially when changes are introduced into the economic system and the educational system.[51] Mobility is also affected by such features of social structure as the relative degree of ascription or achievement, the level of differentiation and the nature of the reward system.[52]

In a relatively undifferentiated system, mobility will be collective rather than individual. Factors influencing mobility can be divided into cultural and social factors. One can legitimately talk about "openness" or "closedness" only after the effects of these two distinct forces have been separated. It is quite conceivable that the higher mobility rates in the Western world can be attributed mainly to social factors and that the real effects of cultural ascription of status can be assessed only after economic expansion and technological innovations have stabilized. Conversely, much of the lower mobility in non-Western so-cieties may be due to cultural ascription which persists to the extent that it discourages social and political change and inhibits the expansion of educational opportunities. Even many educated and skilled persons do not find adequate occupational opportunities due to the slow rate of economic growth. This is more pronounced among those who come from modest family backgrounds and lack political lever-age. Therefore, cultural ascription and level of economic growth are major factors influencing mobility patterns in non-Western societies.

The choice of status dimensions and research methods are crucial in studying mobility rates. In the West, occupational mobility is studied under the assumption mentioned earlier, that one's occupational status reflects one's position in the stratification system. In this tradition, Blau and Duncan argue that ". . . the understanding of social stratification in modern society is best promoted by the systematic investigation of occupational status and mobility. In short, the focus is on the stratified hierarchy of occupations rather than on some other aspects of social differentiation."[53] The validity of this statement clearly lies in its applicability to the Western context; it cannot be generally extended to many non-Western societies. The degree of mobility depends upon the scale of measurement of dimensions. The number of categories that compose a scale affect the amount of apparent mobility; this creates problems in the comparisons of mobility rates between societies. For instance, if the point of destination has a larger number of levels of strata between it and the point of origin, mobility will be apparently greater. It is hoped that meaningful comparable categories can be constructed to solve this problem so that comparable scales can be used to study different societies.

Sociologists have pointed out some other problems in the study of intergenerational occupational mobility.[54] For instance, fathers differ in the number of sons that they have, and the sons of the same father may pursue different occupations. Thus, even though every pharmacist may have a son who is a pharmacist, the number of persons in other occupations whose fathers were pharmacists is increased. The degree of mobility associated with this occupation, therefore, depends on whether one studies it from the father's generational perspective or the son's. The age of fathers at a certain point in time also varies considerably, and this may be related to the measurement of career mobility. There is thus a difficult problem in choosing an appropriate time period when the occupations of fathers and sons can be compared. Some of these limitations also apply to intergenerational educational mobility, particularly the problem of multiple sons of the same father.

THE CONCEPT OF SOCIAL CLASS

The contributions of Marx and Weber on class have already been discussed, and in this section the contemporary understanding of social class in the context of social stratification is briefly outlined. Families can be classified in various hierarchial groupings on the basis of objective or subjective evaluations. Once again conflict and functionalist theorists differ on causes and consequences of social class. The former stress that inequality polarizes groups and that conflicts of interest keep the system constantly in flux. The functionalists, on the other hand, see relative stability as rewards are dispensed according to the contributions made to society. These differing perspectives influence the method of observation and identification of social classes. There are therefore so many definitions of "social class" that it has become almost impossible to use this term without falling into a trap.

Much of the confusion in the definition of social class has been due to the multidimensionality of stratification systems and the desperate attempts on the part of some social scientists to develop a simplistic conception with extensive applicability. Both multidimensionality and the lack of perfect association among the dimensions should convince researchers to adopt a more general and multidimensional definition of social class, without being constrained by the types or the number of classes.[56]

The definition of social class should depend upon the purposes that the researcher has in mind. A clear distinction between social class and social stratification is necessary. Social classes describe real social entities with at least a potential for consciousness of their common situation, while stratification includes a complex of hierarchial differentiations which may or may not be related to any group phenomenon.[57] Therefore, classes may be conceived of as hierarchial groups in the stratification system. The class model in its "open" form rests on the fact that the status attainment process is independent of ascription. It has already been suggested that this is an "ideal type" conception and that there are no known societies where this has been observed. Svalastoga has developed models of differentiation on the basis of "permeability." According to him, "a social system is considered more or less permeable depending upon the ease of entrance to and exit from any position in the system. Thus, a minimum of permeability is indicated when birth determines entrance and death determines exit . . . in other words, permeability is inversely related to the absolute value of the correlation coefficient relating paternal and filial status."[58]

In an idealised "closed" caste model, the permeability is zero, and in an "open" class model, 40 percent or higher. In contemporary industrial societies it is about 80 percent and the correlations among the stratification variables are about .5.[59] The measurement of permeability is quite useful in differentiating models of stratification systems. It enables one to bypass the definitional problems of social class but it does not help much in understanding the social basis of inequality. It is more useful for comparing profiles of stratification systems across national boundaries and in various historical epochs.

There are some methodological constraints on researchers developing strategies for studying social class. It may be possible that not all persons in a society can identify themselves and others as belonging to meaningful classes. In smaller communities it may still be possible that most people have some notion of their general positions in relation to others and also some reasonable understanding of the number of classes, but in larger communities this may not be feasible. The number of classes which are identified and the delineation of boundaries are influenced by the value system of the subject society.

It is possible that a researcher and his respondents may not agree on the number of classes or on the boundaries of those agreed upon. One way of attempting to solve this problem is by developing an index on the basis of objective criteria which can be used to define classes. But if such classes are being related to some other phenomena, then it is possible that the various components of the index may not be identically related to the dependent variables. Another problem with such objective measures is that they do not take into account life-style variables that are ". . . reflected in social participation, residential area, house type, living room equipment and other visible aspects of status which serve to arrange the population hierarchically, if not to segregate it into classes."[60]

If objective status variables are salient, then they should be positively associated with life-style variables. However, the degree of association between these two sets of variables required by the researchers may vary on the basis of their conceptualization of social class and the purpose behind that conception.

The concepts and principles we have discussed have been extensively used in the study of stratification of Western societies. But they are not culture-bound and they can be applied elsewhere. In Western societies achievement exerts greater influence than ascription on the stratification system, and the converse may be found in non-Western societies. More specifically, occupational status may explain a greater proportion of variance in the stratification system in Western societies than in non-Western societies, but there is no reason why it should not be used in the latter as one of the dimensions of the stratification system. All one needs to do is to examine whether occupational prestige is comparable over time and across societies before various stratification systems are compared. The use of concepts and methods with necessary modifications to suit the local cultural conditions would enable us to understand better how various types of stratification systems are created, maintained and changed.

The diversity of Indian society necessitates that researchers adopt a flexible approach to study stratification. Neither a caste model nor a class model would suffice. Both ascriptive and achievement principles operate, and it is the task of the social scientists to investigate the interplay between them. Similarly, functionalist and conflict influences operate simultaneously in varying degrees in determining the emerging stratification system. For instance, in preindependent India the larger landowners monopolized political power and influence. Recruitment to leadership positions was mainly on a hereditary basis. But if the prospective leader was a minor or was considered incapable of maintaining law and order or lacked the ability to interact with outsiders, generally his closest relative was invited to fill the position. During the postindependence period, some of the newly important criteria for leadership positions are skills in settling local disputes, contacts with politicians outside the community and larger political institutions, knowledge of the law and the courts, and the ability to interact with district-level government officials. Despite these new criteria, landownership and family background remained relevant. In other words, both ascriptive status and performance criteria have been used. However, their relative importance seems to be changing.

In Part II, the Indian stratification system is examined and an attempt is made to demonstrate the usefulness of some of the concepts and theories discussed earlier. Some additional concepts are also introduced in the next section. Both sets of concepts are used to study the changes in the stratification system of three Indian communities between 1930–1965.

NOTES

1. Neil J. Smelser and Seymour M. Lipset, "Social Structure, Mobility and Development," in *Social Structure and Mobility in Economic Development*, eds. Neil J. Smelser and Seymour M. Lipset (Chicago: Aldine Publishing Company, 1966), pp. 23–29.

Michael Smith, "Pre-industrial Stratification System," in *Social Structure and Mobility in Economic Development*, eds. Smelser and Lipset, pp. 175–176.

Bert F. Hoselitz, "Interaction Between Industrial and Pre-industrial Stratification Systems," in *Social Structure and Mobility in Economic Development*, eds. Smelser and Lipset, pp. 177–193.

2. Peter M. Blau and Otis D. Duncan, *The American Occupational Structure* (New York: John Wiley & Sons, Inc., 1967), pp. 5–10.

Joseph A. Kahl. "Introduction," in *Comparative Perspectives on Stratification:*

Mexico, Great Britain, Japan, ed. Joseph A. Kahl (Boston: Little, Brown and Company, 1968), pp. x–xi.

Alex Inkeles and Peter H. Rossi, "National Comparisons of Occupational Prestige," *American Journal of Sociology* 61 (1956): 329–339.

Robert W. Hodge, Donald J. Treiman and Peter H. Rossi, "A Comparative Study of Occupational Prestige," in *Class, Status and Power: Social Stratification in Comparative Perspective,* eds. Reinhard Bendix and Seymour M. Lipset (Glencoe, Illinois: The Free Press, 1966), pp. 309–321.

David M. Lewis and Archibald O. Haller, "Rural-Urban Differences in Preindustrial and Industrial Evaluation of Occupations by Adolescent Japanese Boys," *Rural Sociology* 29 (1964): 324–329.

3. Gerhard E. Lenski, *Power and Privilege: A Theory of Social Stratification* (New York: McGraw-Hill Book Company, 1966).

4. Karl Marx, "On Class," in *Structured Social Inequality: A Reader in Comparative Social Stratification,* ed. Celia S. Heller (New York: The Macmillan Company, 1969), p. 15.

5. Ibid., p. 14.

6. Ibid., p. 2.

7. Ralf Dahrendorf, *Class and Class Conflict in Industrial Society,* (Stanford: Stanford University Press, 1959), pp. 19–21.

8. Thomas E. Lasswell, *Class and Stratum: An Introduction to Concept and Research* (Boston: Houghton Mifflin Company, 1965), p. 39.

9. Heller, *Structured Social Inequality,* p. 9.

10. For a detailed commentary on class consciousness see Reinhard Bendix and Seymour M. Lipset, "Karl Marx's Theory of Social Classes," in *Class Status and Power: Social Stratification in Comparative Perspective,* eds. Bendix and Lipset, pp. 6–11.

11. Bendix and Lipset, "Karl Marx's Theory of Social Classes"; Dahrendorf, *Class and Class Conflict in Industrial Society,* pp. 3–25.

Bernard Barber, *Social Stratification: A Comparative Analysis of Structure and Process* (New York: Harcourt, Brace, World, Inc., 1957), pp. 52–54.

12. Hans H. Gerth and C. Wright Mills, eds. *From Max Weber: Essays in Sociology* (New York: Oxford University Press, 1958), pp. 181–182.

13. Ibid., p. 183.

14. A. M. Henderson and Talcott Parsons, eds. *Max Weber: The Theory of Social and Economic Organization* (New York: The Free Press, 1964), pp. 425–428.

15. Ibid., pp. 425–426.

16. Gerth and Mills, eds. *From Max Weber,* pp. 183–184.

17. Ibid., pp. 186–188.

18. Henderson and Parsons, eds. *Max Weber: The Theory of Social and Economic Organization,* p. 428.

19. Gerth and Mills, eds. *From Max Weber,* pp. 189–193, 396–408.

20. Ibid., pp. 194–195.

21. Kingsley Davis and Wilbert E. Moore, "Some Principles of Stratification," *American Sociological Review* 10 (1945): 242–249.

22. Ibid., p. 243.

23. Ibid., p. 243.

24. Talcott Parsons, "A Revised Analytical Approach to the Theory of Social Stratification," in *Class Status and Power: A Reader in Social Stratification,* eds. Reinhard Bendix and Seymour M. Lipset (Glencoe, Illinois: The Free Press, 1953), pp. 92–128.

25. Talcott Parsons, "Equality and Inequality in Modern Society, or Social Stratification Revisited," in *Social Stratification: Research and Theory for the 1970's,* ed. Edward O. Laumann (Indianapolis: The Bobbs-Merrill Company, Inc., 1970),

pp. 13–72.

26. Ibid., p. 19.

27. Melvin M. Tumin, "Some Principles of Stratification: A Critical Analysis," *American Sociological Review* 18 (1953): 387–394.

28. Talcott Parsons, "Equality and Inequality in Modern Society, or Social Stratification Revisited," in *Social Stratification: Research and Theory for 1970's*, ed. Laumann, p. 19.

29. Dennis H. Wrong, "The Functional Theory of Stratification: Some Neglected Considerations," *American Sociological Review* 24 (1959): 772–782.

John Porter, *The Vertical Mosaic: An Analysis of Social Class and Power in Canada* (Toronto: University of Toronto Press, 1965), pp. 16–17.

Arthur L. Stinchcombe, "Some Empirical Consequences of the Davis-Moore Theory of Stratification," in *Class Status and Power: Social Stratification in Comparative Perspective*, eds. Bendix and Lipset, pp. 69–72.

30. Porter, *The Vertical Mosaic*, p. 16.

31. Ibid., p. 17.

Dennis W. Wrong, "The Functional Theory of Stratification: Some Neglected Considerations," pp. 774–775.

Wlodzimierz Wesolowski, "Some Notes on the Functional Theory of Stratification," in *Class Status and Power: Social Stratification in Comparative Perspective*, eds. Bendix and Lipset, pp. 68–69.

32. George A. Huaco, "The Functionalist Theory of Stratification: Two Decades of Controversy," in *Readings on Social Stratification*, ed. Melvin M. Tumin (Englewood Cliffs, N.J.: Prentice-Hall, Inc., 1970), pp. 411–412.

33. Kingsley Davis, *Human Society*, (New York: The Macmillan Company, 1948), pp. 369–370.

34. Ibid., p. 364.

35. Ibid., pp. 386–389.

36. Huaco, "The Functionalist Theory of Stratification: Two Decades of Controversy," p. 419.

37. Lenski, *Power and Privilege*, p. 17.

38. Ibid., pp. 18–19.

39. Ibid., p. 19.

40. Ibid., pp. 20–23.

41. Ibid., pp. 24–42.

42. Thomas E. Lasswell, "Social Stratification: 1964–68," *The Annals of the American Academy of Political and Social Sciences* 384 (1969): 105–106.

43. Lenski, *Power and Privilege*.

44. Kaare Svalastoga, *Social Differentiation* (New York: David McKay Company, Inc., 1965), p. 10.

45. Gerth and Mills, eds. *From Max Weber*, pp. 180–195.

46. Claudio Stern and Joseph A. Kahl, "Stratification Since the Revolution," in *Comparative Perspective on Stratification*, ed. Kahl, p. 15.

Rainer C. Baum, "On Political Modernity: Stratification and the Generation of Societal Power," in *Perspective on Modernization*, ed. Edward B. Harvey (Toronto: University of Toronto Press, 1972), pp. 22–49.

47. Gerhard E. Lenski, "Status Crystalization: A Non-Vertical Dimension of Social Status," *American Sociological Review* 19 (1954): 405–413.

Gerhard E. Lenski, "Social Participation and Status Crystalization," *American Sociological Review* 21 (1956): 458–464.

Elton F. Jackson, "Status Consistency and Symptoms of Stress," *American Sociological Review* 27 (1962): 469–480.

48. Pitirim Sorokin, "Social Mobility," in *Structured Social Inequality*, ed. Heller, p. 317.

49. Ibid.

50. Pitirim Sorokin, *Social Mobility* (New York: Harper and Row, 1927), pp. 139–158.

51. Smelser and Lipset, "Social Structure, Mobility and Development," in *Social Structure and Mobility in Economic Development*, eds. Smelser and Lipset.

Jean Floud, "The Educational Experience of Adult Population of England and Wales as at July 1949," in *Social Mobility in Britain*, ed. D.V. Glass (London: Routledge and Kegan Paul, Ltd., 1954), pp. 98–99.

52. Smelser and Lipset, "Social Structure, Mobility and Development," in *Social Structure and Mobility in Economic Development*, eds. Smelser and Lipset, pp. 12–16.

53. Blau and Duncan, *The American Occupational Structure*, p. 5.

54. Otis D. Duncan, "Methodological Issues in the Analysis of Social Mobility," in *Social Structure and Mobility in Economic Development*, eds. Smelser and Lipset, pp. 51–97.

Melvin M. Tumin and Arnold S. Feldman, "Theory and Measurement of Occupational Mobility," *American Sociological Review* 22 (1957): 281–288.

Saburo Yasuda, "A Methodological Inquiry into Social Mobility," *American Sociological Review* 29 (1964): 16–23.

55. Lasswell, *Class and Stratum*, pp. 19–68; "Social Stratification: 1964–68," pp. 107–109.

Barber, *Social Stratification*, pp. 72–79.

Svalastoga, *Social Differentiation*, pp. 53–54.

56. Lenski, *Power and Privilege*, pp. 74–75.

57. Seymour M. Lipset, "Social Class," in *International Encyclopedia of the Social Sciences*, ed. David L. Sills (New York: The Macmillan Company and The Free Press, 1968), Vol. 15, p. 298.

58. Svalastoga, *Social Differentiation*, pp. 39–40.

59. Ibid., pp. 40–69.

60. Robert W. Hodge and Paul M. Siegel, "The Measurement of Social Class," in *International Encyclopedia of the Social Sciences*, ed. David L. Sills (New York: The Macmillan Company and The Free Press, 1968), Vol. 15, pp. 316–325.

within the system without destroying it. Davis has aptly observed that ". . . the Hindu attempt to construct a system of absolute social inequality is inherently contradictory. . . . A change of occupation, a shift of economic fortune, an alteration in the observance of moral rules and taboos — any or all of these will affect the standing of the group in the eyes of the general community."[8]

MOBILITY IN THE CASTE SYSTEM

It is clear that although the positions of various castes in the local ritual structure tend to be relatively fixed, they can be altered under certain conditions. In order to understand mobility within the ritual structure we will briefly examine the concepts of Sanskritization and Westernization.[9] The term Sanskritization was used by Srinivas in his study of the Coorgs in South India. The concept is described as follows:

> The caste system is far from a rigid system in which the position of each component caste is fixed for all time . . . A low caste was able, in a generation or two, to rise to a higher position in the hierarchy by adopting vegetarianism and teetotalism and by Sanskritizing its ritual and pantheon. In short, it took over, as far as possible, the customs, rites and beliefs of Brahmins and the adoption of the Brahminic way of life by a low caste seems to have been frequent, though theoretically forbidden. This process has been called Sanskritization . . .[10]

In other words, Sanskritization generally means the emulation of brahminical life-styles by lower castes who wish to raise their ritual status. There is more than one model of high status emulation. Besides the Brahmin model, Kshatriya and Vaishya models are accepted as alternatives by the lower castes. According to Srinivas, sometimes even Brahmin residents in villages dominated by non-Brahmin castes may borrow the speech and life styles of the latter.[11] Srinivas reports from his Coorg study that this is more likely to happen in rural areas than in urban centers. He observes that away from the centers of the great tradition, the brahminical way of life tends to approximate the way of life of the dominant caste in the community.

The process of Sanskritization involves mobility within the framework of the caste system. Theoretically, a caste may improve its ritual rank without economic and political power; however, such instances are infrequent. Mandelbaum outlines certain stages through which a caste must pass in the process of social advancement (i) It must acquire objective conditions for high status, primarily wealth; (ii) it must adopt cultural practices associated with the higher ranks, and (iii) it must out-maneuver external opposition to new rank, while maintaining internal unity.[12] Although higher economic status helps improve social rank, there are limits beyond which the process may not be effective. Both Mandelbaum and Srinivas assert that the lower castes, such as untouchables, may not be able to cross certain barriers.[13] The higher castes, even during British rule, were able to reap more benefits from educational and other opportunities than the lower castes. Therefore, the very low castes may find the process of Sanskritization, as a mechanism for improving social status, less attractive and practical.[14]

The process of Westernization is an alternative for those who find the process of Sanskritization too slow and uncertain. Westernization is derived from the changes in technology, institutions, ideology and values which resulted from British influence on Indian society and culture.[15] It may involve such practices as eating beef or pork, consuming liquor, wearing western clothes, smoking pipes as opposed to cigarettes, acquiring a western education, participation in nontraditional occupations, and using western medicine or technology, such as radios, electricity, etc. Westernization therefore involves the adoption of some of those customs and practices that are associated with the British in India. Many of these customs are at variance with the life styles of higher-caste culture, but they have been accepted by many higher castes themselves, especially the educated elites, as they present channels of mobility outside the caste system. Sanskritization and Westernization are therefore, linked and show wide variations in their relationships.

Another important concept that needs introduction at this point is that of the Dominant Caste, which has been useful in describing the political reality in Indian villages. According to Srinivas, a caste is dominant when it is capable of exercising economic or political power and occupies a significantly higher position in the caste hierarchy.[16] A caste that is small numerically but strong economically or politically, or that has considerable numerical strength but lacks high economic power or ritual status may be dominant. The former pattern can be called traditional dominance and the latter, contemporary dominance. The latter type has become important as a result of adult suffrage in the new democratic political process. It is possible for a lower caste to be dominant in a village where higher castes are also present. The relevance of Dominant Caste is even greater since independence when local institutions were created to play a greater role in local planning and development. The success of governmental programs often depends on the cooperation of these dominant groups. They may also take greater advantage of new opportunities for becoming richer and politically more powerful than other groups. Dube suggests that a caste may enjoy most essential elements of dominance but still be far from reaping many implied advantages.[17] This is likely to occur when a dominant caste is divided into opposing factions and uses its resources in internal showdowns. This problem suggests the possibility of specifying conditions in which certain elements of dominance will be more relevant than others, but does not cast doubt on the usefulness of the concept itself.

The foregoing discussion of the concepts of Sanskritization, Westernization, and Dominant Caste indicates that the Indian caste system has been flexible and that stratification should be studied from a multidimensional perspective. A review of some of the important research on rural stratification in various parts of India seems essential. There are many studies that are not reviewed here because they deal with other aspects of rural life and are not relevant to the subject matter of this volume. Our purpose is to present the state of knowledge of stratification in rural India, and no claim is made that all relevant research has been reviewed. It can be safely said that despite a proliferation of empirical studies, systematic examination of changes in the stratification system is lacking.

CASTE AND OCCUPATION

Many researchers report that in contemporary India caste continues to be an important aspect of stratification.[18] It is a major basis for social organization, and much of the interaction in rural settings is governed by caste hierarchies. Caste stratification is elaborately exhibited on ceremonial occasions; in more secular areas its importance may be only secondary. Generally, a caste followed a traditional occupation, but only a few occupations were monopolized by certain castes and often several castes followed a single occupation. For instance, agricultural occupations had members from several castes. The traditional occupations formed a prestige hierarchy based on their distance from pollution-tainted activities and skills. But over the past decades, various nontraditional occupations have emerged and many practitioners of traditional occupations did not feel obligated to serve their clients when more lucrative opportunities were within their reach.

Srinivas reported that in the village of Rampura in Mysore, all castes have traditional occupations, although most people do not follow them.[19] Except at lower-caste levels, people participate in petty trade and business. Some have moved to agricultural occupations from lower occupations. One reason for this mobility is that the village cannot support the increasing population if various castes continue to depend solely upon their traditional occupations. Population pressure and the inability of villages to provide economic support to various caste groups necessitate their movement to towns, where they take up new occupations and subsequently may try to change their caste ranks.[20]

Dube, in his study of Shamirpet in the state of Andhra Pradesh, found that traditionally each caste performs a task in the economic system which has been its major source of livelihood.[21] Except for agriculture, most traditional occupations continue to be monopolized by certain castes. However, the trend is towards the lessening of functional specialization and interdependence between various occupational groups. This trend stems from urban contacts, education, and above all, the opportunity to do and to be something "better." Beals, in another Mysore village, found that the new forces of change have provided alternative occupations in which various castes participate. He concluded that occupational specialization by different castes has become progressively less capable of providing a basis for an economic and social hierarchy.[22] Similar processes have been observed by Sivertsen in a Tamil Nadu village.[23] He found that non-Brahmin castes have been able to improve their status in recent years, mainly due to diversification of the economy.

Beteille reported from Tamil Nadu and Mayer from Central India that most people in the villages they studied were following caste-free occupations, both within the village and outside it.[24] Hitchcock found, in a village in the state of Uttar Pradesh, a movement of several castes away from traditional occupations; however, he noted that the high-caste Rajputs were not happy with the situation. Some of them denounced their own castemen who were engaged in petty trade, manual labor, or worked on their own plots.[25] Shah and Shroff observed that certain castes in a village in Gujarat abandoned their low traditional occupations in an effort to improve their ritual rank.[26] In two other villages in West Bengal and Uttar Pradesh, many castes have changed their traditional occupations due to increased education and greater contact with the outside world.[27] The low-caste Chamars in the Uttar Pradesh village are now largely dependent upon occupations which have not been traditionally assigned to them, and some of them are working as unskilled laborers in the factories around the country.

On the basis of these studies, we can suggest that traditional occupations in Indian villages are being abandoned by many of those who once practiced them. Factors such as the increase in population, emergence of urban and industrial centers, fragmentation of landholdings and decrease in the relevance of traditional occupations themselves have facilitated the participation of various castes in nontraditional occupations. Though these changes may be indicative of greater mobility within the caste system, they cannot be interpreted as signs of the disappearance of the caste system itself. There is sufficient evidence that caste-free occupations are emerging and that persons with varying caste status can be found in similar occupations.

THE DIMENSIONS OF STRATIFICATION

The concepts of Sanskritization, Westernization, and Dominant Caste present a more dynamic view of caste stratification and the lack of intergenerational stability in traditional occupations provides new clues to an emerging stratification system. Indian stratification is not only multidimensional, but individuals and groups make deliberate attempts to take advantage of alternatives in improving their positions in the system. Three stratification dimensions that are frequently identified are caste status, economic status, and political power; while each affects the others, their interrelationships are variable.

Improvement in economic status and political power enhance the process of Sanskritization. Such changes are not always welcome as they create instability in traditional social, economic and political relations. The reactions of the traditionally dominant groups may be to withhold legitimation for the new status seekers. Mandelbaum suggests that the shifting of various ranks has a stabilizing force as it brings ritual rank in line with the realities of economic status and political power.[28] This process enables the system to be responsive to new social changes and integrates new elements to keep the system in a dynamic and adaptive state. Some interesting observations have been made by researchers on this issue.

Marriott reported that Kishan Garhi village has moved into a new era of political and social relations.[29] The influence of old power structures has declined due to the loss of economic power, and lower castes have become more important in the secular affairs of the village. Those castes which have gained wealth have attempted to improve their ritual status and have been helped by caste-raising movements outside the village.

Mayer reported some congruence between caste status and economic status but the relationship was not supported by any caste sanctions.[30] In his study, high castes were found to own most of the land, while lower castes constituted the bulk of the tenants and the labor force. The economic power of the Rajputs (a higher caste) in the village has not, however, been able to repress the strength of the lower castes at the polls. Rajputs have to compete with lower castes for political power. Now, castes below the Rajputs control the power structure of Ramkheri. Mayer reported that Rajputs have started to lower their commensal restrictions in order to recruit new allies from the lower castes, including untouchables.

Bailey found that prior to an increase in trade and the establishment of a new administration in recent years, a village in Orissa experienced a high degree of coincidence between ritual rank, economic status, and political power.[31] However, the present tendency is toward increasing use of economic and political power to improve the ritual

status of some castes, with the notable exception of those at the top
or at the very bottom. The influence of Kshatriyas, for instance, has
declined due to their loss of economic status.

Gough observed in Kumbapettai that until about twenty years ago,
Brahmins owned all the village land, and the rest of the population
worked for them as tenants or laborers.[32] Now, about one-third of the
land has been sold by Brahmins to the people in the nearby town.
Some of the Brahmins are participating in petty trade and business.
The influence of Brahmins has declined not only in the economic
sphere, but in other areas as well. Caste rules have been relaxed, and
lower castes are striving for equality.

Beteille, from his study of Sripuram, reported that until the end of
the nineteenth century, Brahmins dominated the village in all important respects.[33] The emergence of new economic and political institutions in recent decades has challenged the monopoly of the
Brahmins. Non-Brahmin castes are getting more education and participating more and more in the urban-industrial economy. The power
of traditional leaders has declined, and the new political institutions,
such as the panchayat at the village level, have provided the opportunity to various groups for greater political participation. Equality
is more visible in the political realm than in the economic realm, although concentrations of landholdings have declined. The popular
leaders at present are not necessarily the big landowners or of the
highest caste.

Beals noted imperfect relationships between caste status, general
social status, and economic status in his study of Gopalpur.[34] There
are as many wealthy shepherds and farmers in this area as there are
wealthy Brahmins. Caste status is not the only source of wealth and
prestige and several economic strata vary with respect to caste status.
Beteille agrees with Bailey that lower castes face greater difficulties
than higher castes in improving their economic status. An improvement in economic status is crucial for lower castes that are trying to
improve their ritual rank.

Srinivas observed in Rampura that in many instances economic
betterment precedes caste mobility.[35] Those who want to improve
their ritual rank are flexible and determined to acquire whatever is
essential for Sanskritization. For instance, Carstairs noted that the
Yadav and Daroga castes in a Rajasthan village have attempted to
improve their ritual status not only by abandoning their traditional
occupations, but also by entering factory employment with its higher
and more stable income.[36] Similar observations have been made by
Sarma and Sivertsen in their studies. Their research showed, as
Bailey's did, that although ritual status at the top and at the bottom
of the caste hierarchy is fixed, the lower castes are trying to acquire
other sources of prestige, mainly wealth, to improve their ritual

status.[37] While lower castes are improving their social status through increased economic and political power, higher castes are losing power and influence. But they resent less the claim of lower castes to higher rank than they did in the past.[38]

The sense of accommodation of an upwardly mobile, lower caste depends upon the social structure of the community, for under certain conditions, the lower castes may be prevented from improving their status. In a predominantly higher caste village it may take longer for lower castes to alter their traditional statuses. Though the economic power of the Jats is declining in Rampur, the social aspects of the caste's influence have not changed much. The lower castes are not satisfied with their present status.[39] Other studies indicate that little change has occurred in the domination of upper castes and the dependency of lower castes. Singh, in his study of caste tension, reported that the Thakurs (Kshatriyas) continue to dominate the lower castes, despite desperate attempts by the latter to free themselves economically and politically.[40] The persistent humiliation faced by the lower castes is mainly due to their lower economic position. Majumdar reports that the high caste Thakurs of the village Mohana hold the economic and political power and interfere in the day-to-day life of the lower castes.[41] Many of the lower castes have long been helpless under the threats and intimidation of the Thakurs. Some have now begun to resist a little, although they do not seem to be a threat to the Thakurs as yet. Dube finds that though the system of stratification has become more open for the lower castes, the grip of the traditional system is still firm.[42] Therefore, the lower castes must behave with considerable tact and discretion if they seek to enhance their importance. Commenting upon the caste system of Shamirpet, he points out that many castes are entering nontraditional occupations, but that the caste balance has changed very slightly.[43]

THE EXTERNAL FORCES

Many researchers have touched upon the outside influences which have affected the social, economic, and political life of village communities. These outside influences range from land reforms and the establishment of adult franchise to the subtle impacts of education and urban contacts, and have contributed, directly or indirectly, to changes in the various areas of rural life. Many of these factors act together and bring changes, but their relative contributions are difficult to establish. One can understand that the land reforms emancipated many depressed groups from traditional economic and political bondage and that the establishment of new village panchayats based on adult franchise provided new sources of power and prestige, but it is difficult to establish the amount which each of these has contributed to the emergence of a new social organizational principle. It will be worthwhile to review the observations of some of those who have identified these forces.

Adult franchise and the establishment of panchayats have provided new opportunities for castes to act as pressure groups and bargain with each other in various matters. This has facilitated the emergence of new leadership in the villages. The creation of local bodies on the basis of adult franchise has linked the village politically with the larger political system. The new opportunities for numerically dominant groups have created resentment in those groups that controlled the village at one time on the basis of traditional economic and power relations. The higher-caste monopoly of mediation in village disputes has declined and lower castes have begun to assert their right to participation in the decision-making process. Still another force that has undermined the economic dependence of lower castes and the poor on other castes has been the new economic opportunities in rural areas as well as in nearby urban centers. Those who exploit the economic resources and take advantage of new occupational opportunities have less fear of the traditional authority of the Brahmins and Kshatriyas. This should not imply that new opportunities have decreased caste consciousness or made the caste system disappear, but that they have opened more avenues to competition for power and prestige on behalf of many groups that were excluded in the past.

The studies mentioned above also show that caste is an important theme in the study of Indian villages and quite relevant to the new patterns of stratification. The rigid ideas regarding pollution are changing. Many castes deliberately violate the traditional rules and do not fear severe punishment. The lower castes are demanding equality in secular areas although they do not seem to be highly committed to the destruction of the caste system itself. There is also a generational gap in this context. The younger men of lower caste status are more assertive than their elders about their new rights and privileges. If they are numerically dominant this attitude becomes even stronger. Such feelings have often contributed to greater caste solidarity which is expressed in block voting and establishment of caste-based cooperatives, journals, etc., that are supposed to serve the interests of respective castes. Many castes are trying to Sanskritize their ways to improve their ranks while taking advantage of new economic and political opportunities.

The blending of the old and the new, which has facilitated mobility through the idiom of caste, and even change in ritual status, would not seriously undermine the caste system as it was discussed earlier, when considering the concepts of Sanskritization and Westernization. It simply indicates that caste barriers have crumbled, but the system continues to exist. The traditional conception of the caste system has weakened, but there is ample evidence that caste is still the most important basis of identity and interaction. There is no doubt that secular and rational rather than traditional principles are being used in economic competition, and that the occupational structure has become more heterogeneous in terms of caste than ever before. Numerical dominance is more skillfully exploited in the exercise of power. These factors do not in themselves destroy the caste system and though the newly rich and powerful castes have tried to improve their ritual ranks, many of them have not favored the abolition of the caste system.

In conclusion, it can be said that the caste system has been changing during the past few decades, but we do not have any conclusive evidence of its disappearance yet. It is true, however, that criteria of general status have changed and that this has not happened at the expense of caste status. Mason rightly points out that "In India, the number of scales of reference is increasing; wealth, education, political power, international sophistication: all are more and more used not as alternatives but as additional indicators of prestige in different situations. They have come to join caste, knowledge of the sacred Scriptures, ownership of land, ability to reconcile disputants — the traditional means of winning esteem."[44] There is a change from the traditional system of stratification to other and more complex forms of stratification.

CASTE AND CLASS

The members of a caste share equal ritual status, but may differ in their economic power, political influence, education and life-styles. One may suggest that there are classes within castes, but there are formidable obstacles in defining them. Economic criteria are not suitable for determining class boundaries, because caste loyalties interfere in the allocation and acquisition of resources. For instance, it is difficult for the lower-caste person to buy land from an upper-caste person because the latter would have negative sentiments toward the former's attempt to improve his economic status. The seller does not operate solely on market principles in such a case, but largely on sentiment and symbolism. He is more influenced by the fact that a lower-caste person is trying to better himself economically vis-a-vis many higher-caste families and consequently undermining the traditional system. He may still sell the land to this person, however, if he fails to find a higher-caste buyer. Even so, the overall sentiment is generally consistent with the traditional norms according to which lower castes are supposed to work for higher ones and be economically dependent on them.

Attempting to define classes on the basis of political power is fraught with problems. In the contemporary context, election or appointment to political office does not necessarily reflect the power actually exercised by a particular leader or group of leaders. Many de facto officials lack political skills, economic resources and the higher-caste status that are essential for political credibility. Many villagers and outsiders are accustomed to establish contact with high-caste, unofficial leaders to get things done. During this period of rapid social change, the distribution of elected officials among castes is not a satisfactory objective criterion of political power.

A considerable amount of land reform legislation was implemented in India after independence. Prior to the establishment of these laws, on the basis of ownership of property, three social classes were identified by Rosen: those families who owned more than 15 acres, those who owned between 5 and 15 acres, and smaller landholders and landless laborers.[45] The highest class consisted of higher-caste landlords and some dominant-caste families. The second class lived at the subsistence level and did not have the resources or skills to make sufficient improvements in their agricultural operations, although they produced more per acre than the highest class. They were characterized by a heterogeneous caste background and were aware of the new opportunities arising from various social, economic and political changes. The lowest class did not have sufficient land for subsistence and sought employment outside agriculture. They were predominantly lower-caste people.

In a more recent study of Sripuram in 1961–62, Beteille designated landowners, tenants and agricultural laborers as the three classes constituting the class system of the village.[46] The relationships between these classes were influenced by land reform laws as well as by local traditions. Although Both Rosen and Beteille conceptualized ownership of property as the basis for the class structure of rural India, the class lines are drawn differently. The intervening independence of India and the subsequent land reforms are not related to the differences. For instance, in certain areas of the country, renting land to others for an extended period of time is legally discouraged, and therefore the tenant and landlord relationship is often not acknowledged, making it more confusing to attempt to apply Beteille's more recent criteria.

It has been suggested that implementation of land reform legislation has affected the class structure and has lessened the power of the uppermost class.[47] It has not prevented the class of ex-landlords and other privileged groups from searching for new loyalties to retain their superior positions. They have become "contact men" in various matters between the government and the people, and ask for political support in return. The middle class of self-sufficient farmers, however, holds the key to the local power structure through its numerical strength and greater participation in village affairs. It is in a good bargaining position but is often weakened by being divided into factions. Because of its large vote, it also has access to local political representatives and utilizes these contacts to its fullest advantage.

The fate of the lowest class — small landholders and nonowners of property — depends upon its ability to take advantage of outside employment opportunities and to use its numerical strength in local politics for whatever it can get. Its low-caste status tends to limit its social mobility, but those individuals who have the motivation to get organized politically within the village or to work as laborers outside, can sometimes improve their position in the local class structure.

The preceding notion of classes based on the ownership of property is consistent with the Marxian and Weberian conceptions. However, population pressures, the increasing importance of education, the emergence of new urban and industrial occupations, and new opportunities for trade and business as a result of improved transportation and communication facilities have all provided viable alternatives for acquiring wealth or property not derived from land ownership. Unskilled wage laborers may earn more by working outside the village than do villagers who are tied to small landholdings. This alternative is especially possible where there are government sponsored construction projects on highways, railways or irrigation. It is not suggested that land ownership is irrelevant to the definition of class, but it is clear that there is an increasing number of other sources of economic power.

The multidimensionality of the stratification system and the economic and political changes in India demand a more general definition of class than one based solely on land ownership. Although many ex-landlords are still economically well-off and frequently dominate the power structure, they can no longer ignore spokesmen of the numerically superior and hence politically significant lower castes.

In the midst of scarcity, those who have the power to distribute the means of subsistence have high prestige in the community. Prior to independence and the implementation of new legislation, landlords could control the incomes of their tenants and thus assure their economic dependency. They could restrain rebelliousness through their influence over the police and other regional administrative officials. Tenants were subject to intimidation and harrassment and had little chance of redress. Their ownership and control of land enhanced their position outside the village, thus making them easily the most powerful group in the community. Landlords were sometimes divided among themselves and had occasional power struggles, but there was no contest at all between the landholders and the agricultural workers. The new order has not only provided the lowest class with alternative means of subsistence, but has also given them the franchise. Not only has the economic power of the landlord diminished, but so has his political influence. Sentiments, habits, and traditions are rapidly replacing land ownership as the chief sources of prestige of the upper class.

Mosca suggested that in all societies there have been a class of rulers and a class of ruled. The ruling class, which is numerically small, monopolizes power and uses various means to manipulate and control the majority.[48] It displays for the majority of the ruled that it performs those functions that are essential for the existence of organized life. It also demonstrates the possession of those qualities that are socially most relevant. The socialization process enables the children of the ruling classs to acquire positions of power with greater ease compared to others who have very little access to the ideas and functions of the ruling class. When an existing ruling class is overthrown it is replaced by another group of men who perform the same functions and who have demonstrated that they can face the new challenge.

Later in his analysis Mosca divides the ruling class into two strata: one actually has the authority to rule, the other carries out the policies of the first group.[49] This distinction is useful in the analysis of the class system during the preindependence period of India when large princely estates had groups of persons that collected taxes and maintained peace and order on behalf of rulers. At the village level, however, a two-class model would be more applicable. A small number of persons acted as spokesmen of their castes, settled disputes, provided legal advice, and dealt with the police, revenue and development officials on behalf of the village. They also served as a link between the village and outside world and influenced voters in various elections. But they may have been recruited by various methods and from diverse backgrounds and interests, and may also have faced different problems in retaining their membership in the ruling class.

One problem that confronts social scientists today is the identification of classes that may be distinguished on the basis of differential access to power, which in turn determines the distribution of the community's resources. Lenski's definition of class is broad enough to be applicable in this context. He defines a class as "an aggregate of persons in a society who stand in a similar position with respect to some form of power, privilege or prestige."[50] This notion of class fits well with the Indian situation — both past and present. The distribution of surplus in the past lay in the hands of few landholders. At present, government agencies are providing a certain amount of resources for agriculture, education, health, sanitation and so on. These resources are distributed through local offices. Some persons have an enormous amount of influence on decisions about who gets what. These are usu-

disputes, but they also have become a new sourc
ficeholders.

The Community Development program which i.
supposed to provide incentive, encouragement, and ,
sources in an endeavor to eradicate poverty, illitera
handicaps which have prevented people from improving
of life. For the success of these programs, it was decided
agencies should withdraw gradually and let local leadership .
the responsibility of operating the program at the village lev . The
programs expanded, and they are being carried out through the village panchayats. Villages under these programs have undergone
changes in their social, economic, and political aspects.

The second criterion specified that villages be exposed to urban
and industrial environments without being a part of them and have
easy access to markets and lower-level administrative centers. These
factors exposed them to the type of influences which were likely to
increase in the future. It is assumed that accessibility to these centers
provided alternative opportunities for greater social, economic, and
political participation. The lower castes could attend caste raising
conferences, read caste journals, meet important political leaders
(some of them belonging to their own caste), ask for political favors,
and try to find the kind of jobs usually available in urban and industrial settings. It was hypothesized that these possibilities would influence the social, economic, and political organization of the villages.

The third criterion required that the villages be as internally
heterogeneous as possible. It was hypothesized that villages which differed in social structural aspects would respond differently to outside
influences and would behave differently if they decided to achieve
similar goals. For instance, it is possible that a predominantly low-
caste village might take greater advantage of various programs of development than a village with greater caste differentiation. On the
other hand, greater homogeneity and solidarity might discourage people from competing for new sources of prestige such as education and
higher occupations. In the case of multi-caste villages, caste rivalries
might prevent consensus on various programs and lead to few, if any,
accomplishments.

The fourth criterion permitted the analysis of mechanisms through
which the social, economic, and political structures of adjacent villages interact and influence one another. For instance, it would indicate whether the members of a particular caste group occupy similar
statuses on various dimensions of stratification in different villages.
It would enable us to observe whether the mobility of a particular
caste in one village influences the mobility of its caste members in
other villages. By using this criterion we tried to maximize the differences between villages as well as the differences within villages

..s time. It has been suggested that factors such as population size, caste structure, land ownership, system of authority, and proximity to urban and industrial centers account for the most relevant diversities between villages in India.[57] There are other differences based upon regional, linguistic, and cultural factors which were not investigated in this study.

The three villages that were chosen are located between sixteen and seventeen miles south of Lucknow, the capital city of Uttar Pradesh. The police station, subdivisional office, block development office, and the nearest village market are all located between four and six miles from them. The main highway, which runs north and south, is located between five and six miles from the villages. Kanpur, the biggest industrial town in the state, is located about 45 miles southwest of them. They are less than a mile from one another, and many people of each village visit the others almost every day. Social and economic relations between the three villages have increased during recent years, although politically no significant change has occurred. For the sake of anonymity, we have given fictitious names to these villages. They are called in this study Jaiti, Ratu, and Bhagu. It should be pointed out that we have used "village" and "community" interchangeably.

THE UNIT OF ANALYSIS

Caste has been used, implicitly or explicitly, as the unit of analysis by many social scientists who have studied Indian villages. In relation to social mobility, a frequent assumption has been that individuals or families cannot dissociate themselves from their caste fellows while competing for higher status. Such attempts may be thwarted if higher-caste members are organized and as a group reject a lower-caste member's claims for higher status.[58] The less wealthy members of a caste share the prestige of the caste leaders of their village.[59] A characteristic conclusion has been that social status cannot be improved outside one's caste group. Still another argument is that even if it is assumed that higher economic status has elevated ritual rank, endogamy and various commensal rules have changed very little. Therefore, individuals or families outside their castes are likely to face difficulty if they attempt to achieve higher ritual ranks. It is suggested again and again that mobility in a caste system must be in the form of group mobility, and when there is mobility, an entire caste experiences it, not an individual or a family.

There are serious limitations in using caste as a unit of analysis. As an essentially ritual status, it is only one of several aspects of stratification, and furthermore, the ritual status of a particular caste may vary from place to place and over time. Castes are often limited to specific regions, and certain caste names in one area may be unknown to people in another. Its use limits the ability to make comparative analyses across time and space. In fact, the comparison of studies which deal with social mobility and use caste as the unit of analysis constitutes a complex problem. There are indications that mobility has occurred, but judgments about its nature and extent are difficult to make. Barber rightly suggests that sociologists would be better off not using caste as a unit of analysis in investigations of the Indian stratification system, since so many local and regional peculiarities preclude consensus as to what the system actually is.[60]

The argument of caste solidarity should also be evaluated. It may be relevant only when one caste confronts another, hostile caste. In the absence of such a situation, one cannot be sure whether caste would be the most important binding force to individuals and families. Castes have been losing their traditional control over their members. Many of their traditional functions have been transferred to such secular organizations as village panchayats and cooperatives. For example, serious disputes within a caste are frequently referred to village panchayats. Caste leaders have become aware of the fact that their decisions are informal in nature and may not be binding upon the disputants if they do not wish to respect those decisions. The use by disputants of such institutions as the police and the courts has increased.

Marriott has identified some forces that impinge upon caste solidarity and has pointed out that growing differentiation of statuses within each caste, increased contact with the outside society, and frequent internal conflicts within the village have made caste councils less capable of exerting social or moral pressures for disciplining their members.[61] The loss of caste culture, once associated with particular occupations and ritual duties, has accelerated the decline of caste solidarity; people with heterogeneous caste backgrounds more and more frequently form alliances and wield political power to serve their personal economic interests.[62] Probably many such persons have realized that in the climate of general scarcity, they should abandon traditional caste solidarity if it prevents the achievement of their economic ends. In other words, caste solidarity may continue to be important only as long as it does not conflict with other personal interests. People of the same caste now compete for status among themselves.

From the foregoing it can be concluded that the use of caste as the unit of analysis is inappropriate for this research. Statements such as caste A has experienced more educational or occupational mobility than caste B would conceal information on educational and occupational mobility *within* a caste or a caste group. Families with large landholdings may be more likely to occupy leadership positions and less likely to show higher occupational mobility across generations than families with smaller landholdings. Caste as such will not be the unit of analysis, but caste status will be used as one of the stratification variables. Often family or kinship is treated as the basic unit of social organization, but the importance of these relationships within a caste system has not been fully explored. The family has generally been seen as an institution which serves to bind people to particular caste statuses. Most researchers have not recognized its role at the community level.

Although caste as such will not be the unit of our analysis, caste norms still play an important part in social, economic and political relations, and therefore caste will occupy a prominent place in our analysis. In analyzing the stratification systems in the three villages, the following types of questions were asked: Firstly, in what ways does a family's caste position relate to its property status and political power? Are the various dimensions of social stratification and the nature and magnitude of their interrelations associated with certain social, economic, political and demographic conditions? Finally, what implications do intergenerational educational and occupational mobility have on the local stratification system?

The system of social stratification generally places families rather than individuals at various levels.[63] The members of a family usually share the position assigned to it within a social context. The success or failure of different family members will enhance or detract from the position of their family. In other words, individual performances are translated into family prestige. Although there is feedback, the most common direction of status is from the family to the individual. This is probably even more accurate for rural areas than for urban and industrial centers, as people in rural areas are more likely to know each other's histories and to make evaluations accordingly.

For the purposes of this study, a family is defined as a set of individuals related by blood, marriage, or adoption who form a single consuming unit and a single producing unit as well. A family as defined here, may or may not consist of more than one nuclear family. Generally, family property is held in common and title to it is in the name of a senior male member. The members of the family share in the fruits of their labor, live under the same roof, and receive food from the same kitchen. Normally the needs of individuals are met jointly, however, private bank accounts may exist. When individual expenses become burdensome or when a breach occurs, division of the family may take place. Common property such as land, money, cattle, house and various household goods are then divided among members. Although families are normally in a continuous process of reorganization, they still constitute the basic units of social stratification.

Inferences about the stratification system of 1930–46 are based on data gathered about the fathers of respondents (heads of households in 1964–65) as well as on observations of social, economic, and political conditions during this period.

The "father data" may not include those who did not have any children if they and their wives were dead at the time of data collection. It may also exclude those without sons who were heads of families. We also excluded from the father data those families whose daughters brought their husbands to the village, where their husbands became the heads of households. This situation was generally more common in the lower castes than in the higher castes.

The data from respondents themselves are the primary sources for determining the stratification system of 1947–65. These data are supplemented by case studies and observations of intercaste relations, panchayat elections, disputes and decision making during the 1947–65 period. Information about the respondents' sons provide data for the contemporary generation and are suggestive of what future patterns might be.

The three villages differed from each other in certain structural characteristics. These structural characteristics (as well as institutional changes outside the communities) will be used to explain intervillage differences in stratification.

Inequality was inferred from differential possessions and/or opportunities; it therefore encompasses the unequal distribution of possessions and privileges and the principles governing such distributions. More narrowly, inequality may mean differences between families with respect to caste status, ownership of property status, political power, level of education, and occupational status. These are the dimensions of stratification used in this research. To measure inequality in some of these dimensions, the size of standard deviations was observed. To compare the extent of inequality within a community in two different time periods, the time period with the larger standard deviation will be considered to have the greater inequality. The greater inequality, in turn, will be interpreted as a greater degree of social stratification.

Other studies of India have reported that caste status, property status, political power, educational status and occupational status were important in affecting the individual's behavior and in determining his position in the stratification system. Interestingly enough, these variables (with the exception of caste status) are frequently used in the stratification studies of other countries as well. It should be emphasized that in India, the expansion of educational facilities and the greater availability of and participation in nontraditional occupations have added greater importance to educational and occupational status.

We will need a more specific approach to social stratification in this study. Social stratification in this study will be taken to mean the process by which and the resulting structure in which families are placed into higher and lower groups with varying degrees of caste status and/or property status and/or political power and/or educational status and/or occupational status. In other words, families are ranked on the caste, property, political, educational, and occupational dimensions. The rankings may be more or less highly correlated. Comparisons of the distribution of caste, property, political, educational, and occupational resources and the nature and magnitude of their interrelationships will indicate the characteristics of stratification across time in the three communities.

After independence, government legislation was passed aiming at social and political change, such as land reforms, removal of untouchability, establishment of statutory village panchayats elected on the basis of adult franchise, and Community Development programs to upgrade the general social and economic conditions and to facilitate greater political participation at various levels. At the time of this study, these forces of change had already intruded into the three communities. These measures have provided alternative principles for social, economic, and political reorganization and have facilitated the evolution of a stratification system based upon somewhat different principles from those that existed before independence. The analysis of relevant case studies of caste, property, and political relations will supplement quantitative analysis or fill the gaps where quantitative data are not available for these two periods.. In other words, inferences will be drawn, using both quantitative and case data, about the degree of inequality in the two time periods in the three communities. The data for 1930–46 is mainly drawn from personal interviews and is often largely impressionistic.

The changes in the degree of inequality per se may not be of great significance in describing the stratification system, unless they are interpreted in the context of the principles governing them. The existence of such principles and their impact will be considered as additional evidence of increasing or decreasing inequality.

One aspect of this research is the effort to discover the importance of caste status in the emerging stratification system in India. In the past, caste status has been positively correlated with property ownership. Higher-caste children have had an advantage in competition for education and for superior occupations. It seems very likely then, that in India as elsewhere, the nature of the stratification system during a given period of time is influenced by the stratification system that preceded it. India's newly developing stratification system, however, suggests that with the passage of time, caste will have less and less influence on property status, political power, educational status or occupational status.

Data on five stratification variables have been obtained over three generations. The generations are analyzed separately to show the evolution of the stratification system. The means and standard deviations of caste status were not comparable over time because people used two different ranking systems. In 1930–46 they used eighteen ranks, whereas in 1947–65 they used only five. Although direct comparisons cannot be made, observations and case studies of intercaste relations are used to show decreasing social inequality. Since it is assumed that the size of landholdings of the families remained approximately the same across time, changes in economic inequality cannot be made on the basis of possession of land, even though means and standard deviations can be compared between the villages. It will be pointed out that the increasing use of modern methods of cultivation by the larger landholders have widened the economic gap between larger and smaller landholders.

The means and standard deviations of leadership status over time and between villages cannot be compared because the nature and sources of leadership between the two time periods are not comparable. During 1930–46, leadership was primarily hereditary; a few leaders who did not live in the village exerted important political influence. But as mentioned earlier, during 1947–65 the power structure of the village was changed through government legislation. Changes in political inequality have been explained by using primarily qualitative data. Greater political participation, more heterogeneous leadership with respect to social and economic background, and greater demand for political justice are seen as indicative of declining political inequality. Case studies of disputes and decision making throw some light on intervillage differences in political inequality.

Mean number of years of education and mean occupational levels are compared to assess the average increase in these two variables over generations in the villages. In the case of education, higher means imply greater amounts of education, while in the case of occupation they indicate greater participation in higher status non-agricultural occupations. Therefore, means and standard deviations are compared over generations and between villages to assess the average increase in education and occupational participation on the one hand and patterns of educational and occupational inequality on the other. An increase in the mean of a stratification variable over time implies that the general level of the population on this stratification variable has been upgraded. An increase in the standard deviation, on the other hand, indicates greater dispersion in the distribution of the variable, greater status distinctions, and greater inequality.

THE DATA

In a study like this, past records can be of immense help. Unfortunately, in the selected villages most relevant written records for the period 1930–46 either did not exist or were not usable due to inconsistencies and incompleteness. A few leaders during the 1930–46 period were still living, and they helped us to get the names of others, but no records existed of the caste-related decisions made during this period.

The land records prior to 1952 could not be used because many titles were not recorded in the proper names. In the zamindari system, each zamindar followed his own style in this matter. The confusion was greatly multiplied by incompetent or unscrupulous village revenue collectors. Since most people could not read or write, discrepancies continued unchecked. Because it was difficult to establish the degree of exactness of public land records, knowledgeable villagers and revenue officials advised us not to use the available records for this study. While private records were maintained by some ex-zamindars, their authenticity was challenged by others. We finally decided against the use of land records which existed prior to 1952. Information on population, age, and education were not used due to administrative reorganization of two villages after independence.

The data for 1947–65 are largely quantitative. The anthropological method of intensive and sustained observation of populations, and survey research methods in which data on families collected through a structured census schedule were used. All heads of households in 1964–65 were designated as respondents and interviewed to gather data on the members in their families: their age, sex, marital status, place of marriage, education, occupation, place of work, leadership status, landholding, agricultural tools and implements, and number and types of cattle and bicycles owned in 1964–65. Data on the ages, education, occupations, and places of work of fathers of respondents were also gathered. Data on the fathers of respondents were obtained from respondents unless the fathers were living at the time of the interview. "Well-informed" persons were contacted to describe social, economic, and political relations within each village during the past thirty-five years. The choice of well-informed persons was arbitrary.

Lists of formal leaders for the period 1947–65 were obtained from the official records of the village panchayats and the cooperative societies for all three villages. These lists included both elected and appointed leaders. Case studies of the procedures for recruitment and decision making of traditional village panchayats as well as of new panchayats were made. These studies helped to clarify both the nature of the traditional power structure and the shifts and changes which took place during the period under study. These methods of data collection were time-consuming and required considerable tact and patience. However, given the circumstances, they proved to be quite appropriate. The actual fieldwork began in March of 1964 and was concluded in May of 1965.

The data for 1930–46 are largely impressionistic and are being used as tenuous bases for making inferences about economic and political inequality over time. The small number of literate families, the existence of a traditional power structure based mainly on ascription, and the lack of reliable data on land limited the possibility of obtaining appropriate statistics. The well-informed persons told us that we could legitimately reconstruct the landholding of 1930–46 on the basis of land data of 1964–65. They argued that the same land had generally been held by the same families during the past several decades, although sometimes the title was in the name of zamindars. Since the abolition of the zamindari system, legal ownership has been changed without much change in the size of the actual landholdings of particular families.

Combining both quantitative and impressionistic data in the description of the 1930–46 social stratification constituted a problem. The quantitative basis for making inferences was more readily available for 1947–65 than for 1930–46. Between 1930 and 1946, only a few families made most of the history in the villages. Therefore, the social stratification patterns of this period was deduced from verbal reports about such factors as power dynamics, informal economic coercion, and the subtle mechanisms through which ritual status was maintained.

NOTES

1. Oliver C. Cox, *Caste, Class and Race: A Study in Social Dynamics* (New York: Doubleday Company, Inc., 1948) , pp. 3–6.

J. H. Hutton, *Caste in India: Its Nature, Function and Origins* (London: Oxford University Press, 1951), pp. 46–70.

Kingsley Davis, Human Society (New York: The Macmillan Company, 1948), pp. 373–379.

Irawati Karve, *Hindu Society: An Interpretation* (Poona, India: Ducan College, 1961), p. 9.

M. N. Srinivas, *Caste in Modern India and Other Essays* (Bombay: Asia Publishing House, 1962), p. 3.

Louis Dumont, *Homo Hierarchicus: An Essay on the Caste System* (Chicago: The University of Chicago Press, 1970), p. 21.

2. Hutton, *Caste in India*, pp. 64–70.

Bernard Barber, *Social Stratification: A Comparative Analysis of Structure and Process* (New York: Harcourt, Brace & World, Inc., 1957), p. 80.

Karve, *Hindu Society*, pp. 41–49.

Dumont, *Homo Hierarchicus*, pp. 65–72.

3. Hans H. Gerth and C. Wright Mills, *From Max Weber: Essays in Sociology* (New York: Oxford University Press, 1958), p. 397.

4. Harold A. Gould, "Castes, Outcastes, and the Sociology of Stratification," *International Journal of Comparative Sociology* 1 (1960): 220–238.

5. Fredrik Barth, "The System of Social Stratification in Swat, North Pakistan," in *Aspects of Caste in South India, Ceylon and Northwest Pakistan*, ed. E. R. Leach, (London, Cambridge University Press, 1960), pp. 113–146.

6. Davis, *Human Society*, p 379.

Barber, *Social Stratification*, pp. 80–81.

7. Ibid., p. 372.

Dumont, *Homo Hierarchicus*, pp. 33–61.

8. Davis, *Human Society*, p. 384.

9. Srinivas, *Caste in Modern India and Other Essays*, pp. 42–62; *Social Change in Modern India* (Berkeley: University of California Press, 1969), pp. 1–88.

10. Srinivas, *Caste in Modern India and Other Essays*, p. 42.

11. Ibid., pp. 9–11.

12. David G. Mandelbaum, "Status Seeking in Indian Villages," (Berkeley: Center for South Asia Studies and Institute of International Studies, University of California, 1968), Reprint No. 270.

13. Ibid., Srinivas, *Caste in Modern India and Other Essays*, p. 18.

14. Edward B. Harper, "Social Consequences of an 'Unsuccessful' low caste movement," in *Social Mobility in the Caste System in India*, ed. James Silverberg, (The Hague: Mouton Publishers, 1968), pp. 36–65.

15. M. N. Srivinas, "A note on Sanskritization and Westernization," *Far Eastern Quarterly* 15 (1956): 481–496.

Srinivas, *Social Change in Modern India*, p. 47.

16. Srinivas, *Caste in Modern India and Other Essays*, pp. 89–92.

17. S. C. Dube, "Caste Dominance and Factionalism," *Contributions to Indian Sociology* 2 (1968): 57–62.

18. Dagfin Sivertsen, *When Caste Barriers Fall: A Study of Social and Economic Change in a South Indian Village* (New York: Humanities Press, 1963), pp. 9–11.

Adrian C. Mayer, *Caste and Kinship in Central India: A Village and Its Region* (Berkeley: University of California Press, 1960), p. 3.

M. N. Srinivas, "The Social System of a Mysore Village," in *Village India: Studies in The Little Community*, ed. McKim Marriott, (Chicago: The University of Chicago Press, 1955), pp. 1–35.

S. C. Dube, *Indian Village* (Ithaca: Cornell University Press, 1955), pp. 34–87.

McKim Marriott, "Multiple Reference in Indian Caste System," in *Social Mobility in the Caste System in India*, ed. James Silverberg, (The Hague: Mouton Publishers, 1968), pp. 105–107.

Alan R. Beals, *Gopalpur: A South Indian Village* (New York: Holt Rinehart and Winston, 1962), pp. 33–35.

19. Srinivas, "The Social System of a Mysore Village," in *Village India*, ed. Marriott, pp. 1–3.

20. Ibid., pp. 16–17.

21. Dube, *Indian Village*, pp. 57–87.

22. Alan R. Beals, "Interplay Among Factors of Change in a Mysore Village," in *Village India*, ed. Marriott, pp. 88–95.

23. Siversten, *When Caste Barriers Fall*, p. 46.

24. Andre Beteille, *Caste, Class and Power: Changing Patterns of Stratification in a Tanjor Village* (Berkeley: University of California Press, 1965), p. 103.

Mayer, *Caste and Kinship in Central India*, pp. 61–63.

25. John T. Hitchcock, "The Idea of the Martial Rajput," in *Traditional India: Structure and Change*, ed. Milton Singer, (Philadelphia: The American Folklore Society, 1959), p 14.

26. A. M. Shah and R. G. Shroff, "The Vahivanca Barots of Gujarat: A Caste of Geneologists and Mythographers," in *Traditional India*, ed. Singer, p. 45.

27. Nirmal K. Bose, "Some Aspects of Caste in Bengal," in *Traditional India*, ed. Singer, pp. 191–206.

Bernard S. Cohn, "Changing Tradition of a Low Caste," in *Traditional India*, ed. Singer, pp. 207–212.

28. Mandelbaum, "Status Seeking in Indian Villages."

29. McKim Marriott, "Social Structure and Change in a U.P. Village," in *India's Villages*, ed. M. N. Srinivas, (Bombay: Asia Publishing House, 1955), pp. 108–115.

30. Mayer, *Caste and Kinship in Central India*, pp. 61–172.

31. F. G. Bailey, *Caste and Economic Frontier: A Village in Highland Orissa* (Manchester: Manchester University Press, 1959), p. 267.

32. Kathleen E. Gough, "The Social Structure of a Tanjore Village," in *Village India*, ed. Marriott, pp. 36–52.

33. Beteille, *Caste, Class and Power*.

34. Beals, *Gopalpur*.

35. Srinivas, "The Social System of a Mysore Village," in *Village India*, ed. Marriott, pp. 15–17.

36. G. Morris Carstairs, "A Village in Rajasthan: A Study in Rapid Social Change," in *India's Villages*, ed. Srinivas, pp. 36–41.

37. Jyotirmoyee Sarma, "A Village in West Bengal," in *India's Villages*, ed. Srinivas, pp. 186–192.

Sivertsen, *When Caste Barriers Fall*, pp. 30–44.

38. Bose, "Some Aspects of Caste in Bengal," in *Traditional India*, ed. Singer, pp. 201–202.

39. Oscar Lewis, *Village Life in Northern India: Studies in a Delhi Village*, (Urbana: University of Illinois Press, 1958), pp. 80–84.

40. K. K. Singh, *Patterns of Caste Tension: A Study of Intercaste Tension and Conflict* (Bombay: Asia Publishing House, 1967), pp. 56–60.

41. D. N. Majumdar, *Caste and Communication in an Indian Village* (Bombay: Asia Publishing House, 1962), pp. 72–78.

42. Dube, *Indian Village*, pp. 165–166.

43. Ibid., pp. 223–224.

44. Philip Mason, "Unity and Diversity: An Introductory Review," in *India and Ceylon: Unity and Diversity*, ed. Philip Mason, (London: Oxford University Press, 1967), p. 16.

45. George Rosen, *Democracy and Economic Change in India* (Berkeley: University of California Press, 1967), p. 33.

46. Beteille, *Caste, Class and Power*, pp. 102–104.

47. Ibid., pp. 110–112.

48. Gaetano Mosca, *The Ruling Class* (New York: McGraw-Hill Book Company, Inc., 1939), pp. 50–69.

49. Ibid., pp. 403–405.

50. Gerhard E. Lenski, *Power and Privilege: A Theory of Social Stratification* (New York: McGraw-Hill Book Company, 1966), pp. 74–75.

51. Robert S. Robins, "India: Judicial Panchayats in Uttar Pradesh," *American Journal of Comparative Law* 11 (1962): 239.

52. Baljit Singh and Shridhar Misra, *A Study of Land Reforms in Uttar Pradesh* (Calcutta: Oxford Book Company, 1964), p. 21.

53. Ibid., p. 27.

54. Ibid., pp. 19–20.

55. Joseph W. Elder, "Land Consolidation in an Indian Village: A Case Study of the Consolidation of Holding Act in Uttar Pradesh," *Economic Development and Culture Change* 11 (1962): 22.

56. Thomas Metcalf, "Landlords Without Land: The U.P. Zamindars Today," *Pacific Affairs* XL (1967): 6–7.

57. S. C. Dube, "A Deccan Village," in *India's Villages*, ed. Srinivas, p. 202.

58. Bailey, *Caste and Economic Frontier*, pp. 270–271.

59. Adrian C. Mayer, "Caste and Local Politics in India," in *India and Ceylon*, ed. Mason, pp. 123–124.

60. Barber, *Social Stratification*.

61. Marriott, "Social Structure and Change in a U. P. Village," in *India's Villages*, ed. Srinivas, pp. 110–111.

62. Mayer, "Caste and Local Politics in India," in *India and Ceylon*, ed. Mason, p. 125.

63. William J. Goode, "Family and Mobility," in *Caste, Status and Power: Social Stratification in Comparàtive Perspective*, eds. Reinhart Bendix and Seymour M. Lipset (New York: The Free Press, 1966), pp. 582–583.

and 1947–65. On the basis of information supplied by these respondents, a hierarchy of castes was developed for each village for the period 1930–46. These hierarchies are presented in Tables III–1, III–2, and III–3. Although there was consensus with respect to the ranking of several castes at the top and at the botom of each hierarchy, slight differences appeared in the ranking of a few castes in the middle ranges. Several respondents expressed the opinion that the ritual ranking of castes for 1930–46 was not difficult because there was little confusion with respect to a caste's place in the local social structure.

An inspection of Tables III–1, III–2, III–3 indicates that the castes at the top and at the bottom show greater agreement across villages than the castes in the middle ranges of the hierarchy. Although the latter's places are arguable, the differences are not great enough to suggest an alternative caste ranking. The physical proximity and the interpenetration of various social, economic and political structures created a sense of larger community in which people of a caste in a village could identify the location of their castes in another village, whether or not that particular caste existed there. For instance, when the Brahmins of Jaiti and Ratu visited Bhagu, they were accorded high ritual respect, even though Brahmins did not exist at any time in that village. Similarly, when the lower-caste Pasis of Bhagu visited Jaiti and Ratu, they were considered closer in ritual status to their counterparts in these villages. The similarity in the rankings between villages and the close ties between them made it possible to develop a hierarchy of castes which would be applicable in all three villages and which would enable us to make comparisons of stratification systems between the villages. The integrated hierarchy of castes is shown in Table III–4.

Tables III–1, III–2, and III–3, and III–4 indicate that the integrated ranking does not significantly differ from the separate rankings; the rankings of the village of Jaiti seemed to be the framework in which the rankings of the other two villages were fitted. The greater number of castes in Jaiti served as a more useful frame of reference. Change in the ritual status of castes takes a long period of time, so respondents had no difficulty in agreeing on a ranking applicable to all three villages during 1930–46. During the period 1930–46, the violations of caste taboos were relatively few, and the local norms were strong.

After six months, contact was once again made with the respondents who were interviewed earlier and they were asked to arrange the local castes in a way that represented the ritual hierarchy for the period 1947–65. Many lower-caste respondents said that it was impossible to assign each caste a unique place in the hierarchy, except for one or two castes at the top and the same number at the bottom. They indicated that the ranking for 1947–65 was different and complex. However, such responses were not characteristic of informants from the higher castes. The respondents suggested that caste peculiarities of each village had declined during the past two decades and that it was more meaningful to develop an integrated intervillage hierarchy of castes.

Table III–1

CASTE HIERARCHY OF JAITI DURING 1930–46,
(WITH TRADITIONAL OCCUPATIONS)

High

      Brahmin (man of learning)
      Kshatriya (warrior)
      Ahir (cultivator and milkman)
      Gareriya (herdsman)
      Kayastha (bookkeeper)
      Behna (weaver and bangleman)
      Barhai (carpenter)
      Kumhar (potter)
      Kanhar (water carrier)
      Teli (oil presser)
      Nai (barber)
      Dhobi (washerman)
      Kori (vegetable grower and tenant cultivator)
      Pasi (toddy tapper and agricultural laborer)
      Chamar (skinner and tanner)
      Dome (scavenger)

Low

Table III–2

CASTE HIERARCHY OF RATU DURING 1930–46,
(WITH TRADITIONAL OCCUPATIONS)

High

      Brahmin (man of learning)
      Kshatriya (warrior)
      Brahambhatt (genealogist)
      Kumhar (potter)
      Teli (oil presser)
      Chaurasiya (vegetable and betel leaf grower)
      Nai (barber)
      Dhobi (washerman)
      Kori (vegetable grower and tenant cultivator)
      Pasi (toddy tapper and agricultural laborer)
      Chamar (skinner and tanner)

Low

Table III–3

CASTE HIERARCHY OF BHAGU DURING 1930–46,
(WITH TRADITIONAL OCCUPATIONS)

High

Kshatriya (warrior)
Kumhar (potter)
Ahir (cultivator and milkman)
Barhai (carpenter)
Behna (weaver and bangleman)
Pasi (toddy tapper and agricultural laborer)
Dhobi (washerman)
Chamar (skinner and tanner)

Low

Table III–4

CASTE HIERARCHY IN THE THREE VILLAGES DURING 1930–46,
(WITH TRADITIONAL OCCUPATIONS)

High

Brahmin (man of learning)
Kshatriya (warrior)
Ahir (farmer and milkman)
Brahambhatt (genealogist)
Gereriya (herdsman)
Kayastha (bookkeeper)
Behna (weaver and bangleman)
Barhai (carpenter)
Kumhar (potter)
Kanhar (water carrier)
Chaurasiya (vegetable and betel leaf grower)
Teli (oil presser)
Nai (barber)
Dhobi (washerman)
Kori (vegetable grower and tenant cultivator)
Pasi (toddy tapper and agricultural laborer)
Chamar (skinner and tanner)
Dome (scavenger)

Low

The caste rankings for 1947–65 posed special problems because many caste members had improved both their economic status and political power, and the likelihood of mobility was more probable in each separate village hierarchy. The importance of keeping ritual hierarchy conceptually separate from other kinds of hierarchies was carefully explained to the respondents. They were told that if a caste claimed a higher ritual status because it had become more powerful economically and politically in recent years, the validity of that claim must be recognized on acceptance by the villagers in general, in order for them to assign a higher ritual status to that caste. In other words, sheer claims of caste members were not sufficient ground for respondents to assign them a higher ritual status than before. Respondents ranked the 1947–65 castes in fewer categories than they had the 1930–46 castes. Some castes were assigned equal rather than unique ritual status. The two upper-caste respondents divided the castes into six and eight categories respectively; respondents from the eleven castes in the middle identified between four and six categories; and the five lower-caste respondents proposed from three to five categories. The upper-caste respondents were obviously more discriminatory; caste members became less and less discriminatory as they were located further down the hierarchy. The lower-caste respondents were least discriminatory; two of them suggested that it was no longer important to rank castes ritually since other factors can discriminate castes more realistically. These two respondents were educated men who held permanent jobs outside agriculture even though they were members of ritually low castes.

The number of categories into which respondents put ritual castes for 1947–65 ranged from three to eight, but the relative position of the castes in each hierarchy was very stable. Only three castes were assigned different relative positions from their 1930–46 ranks. The Muslim caste of Behna which was accorded seventh place during the 1930–46 period, was now placed by most respondents with the castes which had ranks lower than ten. The Nai had ranked thirteenth before, but now it was assigned a place with castes which ranked higher. Although there was substantial agreement about lowering the ritual status of the Muslim caste, some people also questioned the new status of the Nai. A five-fold hierarchical classification of castes in the three villages has been prepared to summarize the ritual rankings for 1947–65.

Table III–5

CASTE HIERARCHY IN THE THREE VILLAGES DURING 1947–65,

High	Caste Categories
	A Brahmin, Kshatriya
	B Ahir, Brahambhatt, Gereriya, Kayastha
	C Barhai, Kumhar, Kanhar, Nai
	D Behna, Chaurasiya, Teli
	E Dhobi, Kori, Pasi, Chamar, Dome
Low	

In addition to Nai, it was noted that Barhai, Kumhar and Kanhar improved their initial status slightly, primarily due to the status loss suffered by Behna. The latter experienced the status loss as a result of decline in the political influence of Muslims in the area after the abolition of zamindari. These changes also contributed to the decline of the ritual statuses of Chaurasiya and Teli. It should be pointed out, however, that the changes in the relative positions were marginal and did not require any dramatic shifts in the norms that governed intercaste relations.

The respondents reported that the ritual distinctions and ritual aspects of caste consciousness had lessened during 1947–65, compared to the earlier period 1930–1946. Traditional occupations and commensal rules were the most important criteria of ritual caste hierarchy. For instance, during the lengthy feasts given by higher castes, in 1930–46, two castes which were ritually unequal were not served together due to the fear of pollution caused by physical contact. In the 1947–65 period, ritual pomp and ostentation diminished and there were fewer feasts, which tended to be short, and all castes were not invited, so there was less opportunity for observing commensal rules. People had become less conscious of pollution; ritual distinctions persisted in 1947–65, but their influence was not as strong as in the past.

Many lower-caste families have refused to perform their traditional lowly occupations in recent years and have avoided ceremonial occasions where they might be reminded of their lower ritual status. They also changed their life-styles. For instance, they abandoned eating dead cattle and tried to adopt strict sexual mores. The upper castes in the three villages surveyed have generally accepted the new trends in lower castes' behavior reluctantly.

Caste groups in the middle, such as B, C, and D in Table III–5, have ambiguous ranking in the ritual hierarchy, and as they are not accepted as peers by caste groups at the top or bottom of the ritual scale, they have been combined to form a single category and are designated as "middle-range castes." Their status in relation to one another is not clearly defined. In identifying them as middle-range castes, we have abandoned rigor for relevance. We have chosen the latter whenever it will help us understand the phenomena of stratification and mobility.

Table III–6 shows that Jaiti is the largest of the three villages studied. It has a total population of 1193, distributed in 224 families. Next is Bhagu with a total population of 401, and 84 families. Ratu is the smallest with a total population of 381, distributed in 71 families. Table III–7 indicates that Jaiti has proportionately more people in the highest caste category than Ratu or Bhagu, and Bhagu has more people in the lowest category (79 percent) than Jaiti (52

percent) or Ratu (62 percent). Regarding the population of middle-
range castes, Ratu has the largest number (33 percent), followed by
Jaiti (25 percent) and Bhagu (17 percent). Bhagu can be designated
as a predominantly low-caste village. Compared to Ratu (5 percent)
and Bhagu (4 percent), Jaiti, with 23 percent of its people in the
highest category of castes can be called a high-caste village. Ratu
falls somewhere between Jaiti and Bhagu, although the majority of
its population is of lower-caste status.

Social structure is related to the number of castes present in a village during a particular period of time. The greater the number of
castes, the more differentiated is the social structure. Generally, the
more differentiated the social structure is, the more stratified the community. A community with a larger number of castes provides a
greater range for ritual observances than a community with a smaller
number of castes. The latter not only has a relatively less differentiated social structure but also a less stratified ritual structure (except
on important ceremonial occasions when specialized castes are invited
from elsewhere to participate in ceremonies).

Table III–6

DISTRIBUTION OF POPULATION IN VARIOUS CASTES
IN THE THREE VILLAGES.

High	Jaiti		Ratu		Bhagu	
	No. of Families	No. of People	No. of Families	No. of People	No. of Families	No. of People
Brahmin	23	163	2	13	—	—
Kshatriya	26	105	1	4	3	14
Ahir	6	31	—	—	1	4
Brahambhatt	—	—	5	51	—	—
Gereiya	4	20	—	—	—	—
Kayastha	3	10	—	—	—	—
Behna	21	118	—	—	3	11
Barhai	6	28	—	—	1	5
Kumhar	7	29	1	1	10	49
Kanhar	3	14	—	—	—	—
Chaurasiya	—	—	6	25	—	—
Teli	2	7	7	30	—	—
Nai	6	49	4	21	—	—
Dhobi	2	12	4	17	1	5
Kori	45	271	14	69	—	—
Pasi	32	158	25	141	50	253
Chamar	35	162	2	9	15	60
Dome	3	16	—	—	—	—
Low						
Total	224	1193	71	381	84	401

Table III–7

DISTRIBUTION OF POPULATION IN VARIOUS CASTE CATEGORIES
IN THE THREE VILLAGES

Caste Categories	Jaiti		Ratu		Bhagu	
High	Number	Percent	Number	Percent	Number	Percent
A	268	23	17	5	14	4
B	61	5	51	13	4	1
C	120	10	22	6	54	13
D	125	10	55	14	11	3
E	619	52	236	62	318	79
Low						
Total	1193	100	381	100	401	100

Note: The caste categories are based on Table III–5.

A comparison of the caste structures of the villages reported for 1930–46 (Tables III–1, III–2, and III–3) indicates that there were sixteen castes in Jaiti, eleven in Ratu and eight in Bhagu. The number of castes designated for 1947–65 remained the same for each village, even though several castes were assigned similar ritual statuses. Despite fewer ritual distinctions, each caste is still quite distinct from every other caste. We maintain that the ritual caste structures in the two time periods have remained the same, because the number of castes in each village has not changed. On a scale of caste differentiation, Jaiti is higher, Bhagu is lower and Ratu is somewhere in the middle.

PROPERTY STATUS

The property status of a social unit is assessed by comparing its possession of the means of production and its accumulation of wealth with those of others. Similarly, the property status of a family is an index of its amount of control over those economic assets which are the sources of its income and also an index of its potential for acquiring the good things of life, however defined by them. Rights and obligations customarily associated with property status determine to some degree the relations between social units.

One way of measuring the property status of a family in an agrarian society is by the size of its landholding.[6] Under the conditions of high unemployment or severe underemployment, the ownership of land becomes perhaps the best indicator of a family's property status. Land is the most precious possession in Indian villages; it is the most stable form of capital investment, and the primary source of income.[7] A family may also possess property in the form of livestock and agricultural implements. A fortunate family may own sufficient land to produce enough fodder and grain to feed not only the bullocks used in their agricultural operations, but also other livestock — cows, buffaloes, pigs, sheep and goats. The kind of livestock raised is more closely related to ritual caste status than the size of landholdings. Certain types of livestock such as pigs and goats are not raised by many families simply because they lower their prestige. Only lower castes raise pigs, a few middle and lower castes raise goats and sheep. Even in Bhagu where raising pigs is common, none of the castes in the middle and at the top ever raise them. There are instances in Jaiti and Ratu where higher castes have discouraged, through various means, some of the middle-caste families from raising goats, sheep and chickens.

Generally, the correlations of landholdings with other forms of property are medium and positive (see Appendix A). However, some specific possessions do not correlate very highly. Others show negative correlations. It is also not possible to accurately assign monetary value to stable possessions. It was found that the respondents would not cooperate in assessing the value of various possessions, under the assumption that these might be used by revenue authorities for tax purposes. The question of monetary valuation of family possessions was therefore dropped.

We found that the best single indicator of a family's property status is landholding. Normally a certain amount of landholding encourages the possession of such livestock as bullocks, cows and buffaloes, which are highly valued. Some of them are used in agricultural operations and others to meet domestic needs such as milk, milk products and dried dung for fuel. However, the possession of bullock carts and chaff cutters in these villages does not correlate highly or systematically with landholding except in Jaiti. In Ratu, there are very few bullock carts and chaff cutters. In Bhagu, there are also few bullock carts, and only one chaff cutter which is owned by a relatively wealthy low-caste family. Families with very small landholdings rarely use a bullock cart as a means of transporting goods to market. The chaff cutter correlates better with the number of animals than with the size of landholdings in both Jaiti and Ratu.

The consumer income of a family is not necessarily a reflection of its property status for it also takes into account income and wages earned from agricultural labor, raising livestock, petty trade, or work outside the village. However, it was found that people who could afford to do so invested their outside income in land unless they were discouraged from doing so by local customs. There are some families in Jaiti, Bhagu and Ratu who have done so. Land is a stable and desirable investment, especially for those who are uncertain of the stability of their nonagricultural jobs.

Tables III–8, III–9 and III–10 show the distribution of land in the three villages. Most of the families who own land do not own very much. Jaiti has relatively more families with larger amounts of land-holdings than Ratu or Bhagu, although the average landholdings in the villages are quite similar. It is interesting to note that Bhagu has fewer families on either end of the scale than Jaiti or Ratu.

The concentration of landholding for the period 1930–46 was estimated from the number of zamindars who owned more than 20 acres of land — the smaller the number of zamindars owning a substantial amount of land, the greater the degree of concentration. Jaiti had five zamindars — two Brahmins, two Kshatriyas, and one Muslim — during 1930–46. The one Kshatriya and two Brahmin zamindars owned between 40 and 50 acres each. The other two zamindars owned between 27 and 33 acres each. Ratu had two zamindars — a Kshatriya and a Muslim. The former owned about 32 acres while the latter owned about 27 acres. The Muslim zamindars of Jaiti and Ratu did not live in the villages but visited them once or twice a year to collect land revenues and settle other matters related to land. Bhagu had only one Brahmin zamindar who did not live in the village, but he owned land in several other villages in the area. About 80 percent of the total land in Bhagu was under his control. Bhagu had, therefore, the greatest concentration of land-ownership; next came Ratu, while Jaiti showed the lowest concentration of all.

Table III–8

DISTRIBUTION OF LAND BY FAMILIES IN JAITI		
Size of Landholdings (in bighas*)	Number of Families	Percentage of Families
0	10	4.46
1	70	31.25
2	42	18.75
3	41	18.30
4	11	4.91
5	25	11.16
6	2	.89
7	3	1.34
8	4	1.79
9	2	.89
10	1	.45
11	5	2.23
12	3	1.34
13	4	1.79
—	—	—
21	1	.45
Total	224	100.00

*One bigha is approximately .66 acre.

Table III–9

	DISTRIBUTION OF LAND BY FAMILIES IN RATU	
Size of Landholdings (in bighas*)	Number of Families	Percentage of Families
0	5	7.05
1	26	36.62
2	14	19.72
3	7	9.85
4	6	8.45
5	4	5.63
6	0	0.00
7	3	4.23
8	2	2.82
9	6	0.00
10	2	2.82
—	—	—
20	2	2.82
Total	71	100.00

*One bigha is approximately .66 acre.

Table III–10

	DISTRIBUTION OF LAND BY FAMILIES IN BHAGU	
Size of Landholdings (in bighas*)	Number of Families	Percentage of Families
0	3	3.61
1	17	20.48
2	20	24.10
3	20	24.10
4	7	8.43
5	6	7.23
6	4	4.82
7	2	2.41
8	2	2.41
9	0	0.00
10	2	2.41
Total	83	100.00

*One bigha is approximately .66 acre.

The concentration of landholding for the period 1947–65 was different, primarily because zamindari was abolished in 1951–52 and many former tenants became owners. Some of the previous village-based zamindars dislodged a few tenants through various means, but most of the tenants succeeded in staying on their land, this time with legal ownership. The degree of concentration of landholding for the period 1947–65 was measured by the percentage of the total land owned by the 5 percent of the families with the largest landholdings. The larger the percentage of land owned by this group, the greater the degree of concentration. Between 1947 and 1965, 21 percent of the land in Jaiti, 27 percent in Ratu, and 15 percent in Bhagu was owned by the top 5 percent of the landholding families in each village. Jaiti, which showed the lowest concentration of landownership during 1930–46, was in the middle during 1947–65, and Bhagu moved from the highest to the lowest concentration. Ratu, which was in the middle, moved to the top in concentration during 1947–65.

During the period 1930–46, the presence of a zamindar in the village was crucial in the exercise of economic controls. Resident zamindars demanded more help, favors and support, and had greater opportunities to interfere in the lives of their tenants. Sometimes they dislodged a few tenants, often temporarily, to get their way, indicating their economic power. Generally, the absentee zamindars gave more protection to their tenants and were involved in local politics. Their major expectation from their tenants was the payment of land revenue; as long as their tenants paid it, the problem of taking away the land rarely arose.

POLITICAL POWER

For the purposes of our research, political power was defined as the capacity (whether exercised or not) of some social units to influence the behavior of other social units. Some social units obviously must have more power than others. Power differences between the social units create power inequality in the community. The political status of a family referred to its access to powerful positions within the community. It was measured by the family's representation in both formal and informal community leadership positions. It is not suggested that families without leaders are powerless; however, families with members in leadership positions have relatively greater political power than families without any such members. In the investigation of power inequality, respondents were asked to identify the informal leadership status of the members of their families. Their identification was generally based upon whether or not members of their families participated in village-wide decisions.

The names of formal leaders were obtained directly from the village records. Formal leadership status was defined as office holding in one or more of the village organizations, such as the new village

panchayats, nyay panchayats and the cooperative societies. The traditional village panchayat which existed during 1930–46 was considered
a formal village organization.

In the three villages surveyed during the preindependence period
leadership was derived from traditional sources. A few families had
held leadership positions for long periods of time in the traditional
panchayat. This situation changed after independence. The system
of adult franchise and the establishment of new local bodies guaranteed entry of several formerly excluded groups to leadership positions.

The number of leadership positions and the number of areas of
leadership increased during 1947–65, compared with 1930–46. During
1947–65, three panchayat elections took place and several formal
leaders were not returned to office in subsequent elections. However,
defeat in an election did not disqualify a family from being considered powerful for the entire period because most of such former formal
leaders played informal leadership roles and influenced village politics even after their defeat.

Leaders were not particularly inclined to generate consensus on
issues. Often they used their influence to enhance or to impede a
decision simply as a part of the dynamics of local factionalism. In
the few instances in which formal leaders did not consult the informal leaders, either the latter saw to it that the decisions were appealed in the higher courts or one of the parties openly refused to
accept them as binding.

Some of the informal leaders were key men who greatly influenced
the mobilization of the people towards Community Development
and Panchayati Raj programs; however, the leaders who were heads
of village panchayats and cooperative societies were more powerful
than most other leaders. The contests for these positions have grown
keener since the first panchayat elections in 1949. The initiative of
panchayat members is decisive in carrying out the programs of
planned change, and they are contacted for various purposes by outside individuals and organizations.

The term "power structure" involves the distribution of both
formal and informal leadership positions within a village. The areas
of village life subject to community decisionmaking by the village leaders increased between 1930–46 and 1947–65. In 1930–46,
village life was so organized that there were fewer disputes
and fewer leaders who had legitimate authority to settle them. During 1947–65, all of the old areas for decision making remained; new
areas such as community projects had been added; and within both
the number of problems which demanded the immediate attention of
village leaders increased.

During 1930–46, both formal and informal leaders were recruited primarily on an ascriptive basis. The formal leaders included the traditional village head (mukhia) and a few influential persons, who constituted the traditional panchayats. The number of persons constituting a traditional panchayat varied between three and five in the villages under study.

The concentration of power is an important aspect of the political structure. It was measured by the proportion of families containing leaders out of the total number of families in the village. The smaller the proportion the greater the concentration.

All zamindars played formal or informal leadership roles. In Jaiti, from 1930 to 1946 there were five formal and five informal leaders, of whom three were not zamindars. Thus Jaiti had ten leaders. The traditional village panchayat in Ratu had three leaders in addition to which there were two informal leaders. Of these five leaders, two were zamindars. In Bhagu there were three leaders in the traditional village panchayat and one informal leader. The latter was the representative of the zamindar. Jaiti had a higher degree of political concentration than Ratu or Bhagu. Bhagu in turn had a greater concentration than Ratu.

These villages differed in their decision-making procedures. In Jaiti it was difficult for lower castes to expect justice if they were involved in a dispute with the higher castes. Some members of a few lower-caste families were driven out of the village because they did not behave in a fashion commensurate with their low status. In Ratu the lower castes were heard and were dealt with more fairly than was usual in Jaiti. Higher and middle-range caste people could be reprimanded on behalf of lower-caste persons. But lower-caste persons were given harsher punishments for similar offenses. Bhagu was a predominantly low caste village, and leadership was shared by both lower and higher castes.

There were 64, 32, and 28 leaders in Jaiti, Ratu, and Bhagu, respectively, during 1947–65. Jaiti continued to have the highest concentration of political power (.28), Bhagu came next (.33), and Ratu had the lowest political concentration of all (.45). It was widely believed that political decisions in the villages had become more democratic than they had been in the past. The higher castes were still favored over the lower castes, but such practices were on the decline. For instance, there were several instances in which people of various castes challenged the most powerful leaders in the villages and refused to comply with their judgments. Sometimes, by appealing to the higher courts, they even embarrassed the high-caste powerful leaders. This was attributed to the new political roles of lower-caste groups in local politics. During this period it became increasingly difficult for a few powerful men to have their way.

EDUCATIONAL STATUS

Educational status in these villages was taken to refer to the number of years of academic training of an individual in an institution of full-time education. Since some of the data for fathers of respondents and respondents themselves were in such forms as "below primary school" or "slightly above primary school" or "middle school failed," we developed the following categories from high to low to organize the educational data:

10th grade and above
6th to 9th grade
1st to 5th grade
None

These categories are each associated with a level of ability to pursue skilled nonagricultural occupations. Those who have achieved the top educational category are considered to be the local elite. Some of them pursue white-collar occupations outside the village. Those families whose heads have completed between six and nine grades are thought of as "educated people"; some of them pursue such occupations as primary school teacher, village record keeper, and clerk. Those who are literate but have not been educated beyond the 5th grade are able to manage their personal affairs where simple reading and writing are involved, but are less likely to pursue occupations in urban and industrial settings. Of course, those who have no education are dependent on those who have education; they are less likely than the educated to break away from the traditional agricultural economy.

According to Tables III–11, III–12, and III–13, the level of education has increased with each successive generation. There were differences in the distribution of education in the three villages during the period 1930–46. During 1947–65, Jaiti and Ratu had similar literacy rates, while Bhagu continued to lag behind. In the third generation as represented by the oldests sons of heads of households, both Ratu and Bhagu had begun to have a majority of males with some schooling, and Ratu even surpassed Jaiti in the number who had attended school. During 1930–46, the level of literacy was quite low in all three villages, but Jaiti had relatively more families with higher levels of education.

Table III–11

DISTRIBUTION OF EDUCATION ACROSS THREE GENERATIONS IN JAITI

Level of Education	Fathers of Respondents (1930–1946) Number	Fathers of Respondents (1930–1946) Percent	Respondents (1947–1965) Number	Respondents (1947–1965) Percent	Sons of Respondents (18 Years and Above) Number	Sons of Respondents (18 Years and Above) Percent
10th Grade & above	1	—	6	3	3	6
6th-9th Grade	5	2	10	4	7	13
1st-5th Grade	36	16	67	29	12	23
None	167	75	141	63	30	58
No information	15	7	—	—	—	—
Total	224	100	224	99	52	100

Table III–12

DISTRIBUTION OF EDUCATION ACROSS THREE GENERATIONS IN RATU

Level of Education	Fathers of Respondents (1930–1946) Number	Fathers of Respondents (1930–1946) Percent	Respondents (1947–1965) Number	Respondents (1947–1965) Percent	Sons of Respondents (18 Years and Above) Number	Sons of Respondents (18 Years and Above) Percent
10th Grade & above	—	—	2	3	—	—
6th-9th Grade	1	1	5	7	7	22
1st-5th Grade	7	10	19	27	15	47
None	55	77	45	63	10	31
No information	8	11	—	—	—	—
Total	71	99	71	100	32	100

Table III–13

DISTRIBUTION OF EDUCATION ACROSS THREE GENERATIONS IN BHAGU

Level of Education	Fathers of Respondents (1930–1946) Number	Fathers of Respondents (1930–1946) Percent	Respondents (1947–1965) Number	Respondents (1947–1965) Percent	Sons of Respondents (18 Years and Above) Number	Sons of Respondents (18 Years and Above) Percent
10th Grade & above	—	—	1	1	—	—
6th-9th Grade	—	—	1	1	2	6
1st-5th Grade	6	7	10	12	16	47
None	61	73	72	86	16	47
No information	17	20	—	—	—	—
Total	84	100	84	100	34	100

OCCUPATIONAL STATUS

Occupational status refers to the type of employment or activity performed by a social unit as its main source of livelihood. Occupational activities not only provide families with a livelihood, but also influence their general status in the community on the basis of the prestige of the occupations they pursue. Studies of occupational prestige in rural India have shown disagreements about the relative prestige of farmers. It is interesting to see that consistent results were obtained at the extremes, with professionals at the top and unskilled manual and agricultural laborers at the bottom.[8]

A group of respondents was asked to arrange eighteen selected occupations in a prestige hierarchy.[9] Farmers were defined as those persons who derive their major source of livelihood from working on their own land. Traditional occupations such as priest, oil presser, barber, potter, herdsman, carpenter, weaver, bangleman, washerman, and tanner were excluded. Most of them worked on small plots of land for subsistence and practiced their trades for supplementary income; they were more representative of preindustrial Indian social and economic systems.

There were some families in these villages which depended upon income from occupations other than farming. Frequent contacts outside the villages provided them with a broader framework for occupational rankings. The respondents suggested the following prestige hierarchy of occupations from high to low:

doctor
engineer
administrative officer and military officer
lawyer and politician
businessman
teacher (primary school)
shopkeeper
clerk
military soldier
driver
postman
policeman (constable)
skilled worker (factory, railways, and construction)
unskilled nonagricultural laborer
farmer (owner-operator)
agricultural laborer

The criteria probably used by most of the respondents in this ranking were the proceeds or income from the occupation, the level of education it required, and the degree to which the job avoided hard physical labor. Of the 18 occupations ranked, none of the villagers themselves participated directly in the top six, but some had direct contacts with others working in them. Since most of the villagers were concentrated in the three occupations at the bottom, it was decided to combine ocupations in eight major categories which were used in another study.[10] The following are the occupational categories, which are arranged from high to low in terms of prestige:

professional, government officer, politician and businessman
teacher
clerical and related worker
service (class IV and police)
skilled worker
unskilled nonagricultural laborer
farmer
agricultural laborer

Some of these categories had only one or two families in them; some held none. Therefore, we collapsed them further into four major categories which were used for constructing transition matrices in the study of intergenerational occupational mobility. The categories finally used, arranged from high to low, are:

professional and white-collar worker
skilled and unskilled worker
farmer
agricultural laborer

Tables III–14, III–15, and III–16 show the distributions of families from the villages by occupational levels.[11] Comparison of these tables indicates that participation in the higher occupations increased across generations in these villages. Bhagu continued to be lowest in its occupational participation outside of agriculture. People from Jaiti and Ratu entered the higher occupations with accelerated rates in the third generation, while in Bhagu no · significant change occurred.

Occupational structure refers to the distribution of the employed male labor force of the village in occupations inside and outside the village. The occupational structure of a village can be measured by the percentage of families engaged in nonagricultural occupations. A higher percentage of the labor force engaged in nonagricultural occupations indicates a more diversified occupational structure and a movement away from the traditional village economy. The agricultural category includes farmers and agricultural laborers and the nonagricultural category consists of unskilled and skilled workers, clerical and related workers, teachers, and business and professional occupations. Participation in nonagricultural occupations has increased since independence and this has changed the occupational structure generally toward greater diversity. But the communities differed in this respect. In Ratu 21 percent of respondents participated in nonagricultural occupations; in Jaiti there were 17 percent and in Bhagu, only 5 percent. There was some participation in the higher occupations too. Five percent of the respondents in Jaiti, 7 percent in Ratu, and 2 percent in Bhagu were engaged in professional and white-collar occupations.

Table III–14

DISTRIBUTION OF OCCUPATIONS (FROM HIGH TO LOW) ACROSS THREE GENERATIONS IN JAITI

| | The Generations | | | | | |
| Occupational Categories | Fathers of Respondents | | Respondents | | Sons of Respondents | |
	Number	Percent	Number	Percent	Number	Percent
Professional and white-collar worker	8	4	12	5	12	23
Skilled and unskilled worker	27	12	25	11	7	13
Farmer	157	70	161	72	32	62
Agricultural laborer	12	5	20	9	—	—
No information	20	9	6	3	1	2
Total	224	100	224	100	52	100

Table III–15

DISTRIBUTION OF OCCUPATIONS (FROM HIGH TO LOW) ACROSS THREE GENERATIONS IN RATU

| | The Generations | | | | | |
| Occupational Categories | Fathers of Respondents | | Respondents | | Sons of Respondents | |
	Number	Percent	Number	Percent	Number	Percent
Professional and white-collar worker	3	4	5	7	5	23
Skilled and unskilled worker	9	13	10	14	3	14
Farmer	46	65	50	70	10	45
Agricultural laborer	5	7	6	8	4	18
No Information	8	11	—	—	—	—
Total	71	100	71	99	22	100

Table III–16

DISTRIBUTION OF OCCUPATIONS (FROM HIGH TO LOW)
ACROSS THREE GENERATIONS IN BHAGU

| | The Generations | | | | | |
| | Fathers of Respondents | | Respondents | | Sons of Respondents | |
Occupational Categories	Number	Percent	Number	Percent	Number	Percent
Professional and white-collar worker	—	—	2	2	1	6
Skilled and unskilled worker	—	—	2	2	—	—
Farmer	67	80	77	92	16	89
Agricultural laborer	—	—	1	1	—	—
No Information	17	20	2	2	1	6
Total	84	100	84	99	18	101

The caste status of a family is determined by the position of its caste in the local ritual hierarchy of castes. Its property status is measured by the ownership of land. The political power of a family is based on its access to formal and informal leadership positions. Level of education is measured in terms of number of years of schooling completed by the senior male of the family, and occupational status is measured by the prestige of the main occupation of the family. Measuring some of these variables was difficult due to the inability of some of the respondents to provide exact information.

The social structural characteristics of the villages were developed by pooling the family data on relevant aspects of the community and then making intervillage comparisons, which enabled us to make qualitative distinctions between the villages. These structural characteristics constitute the social environment in which the stratification system develops and changes. Thus, social structural characteristics can be used to explain the stability or changes in various aspects of a stratification system across time in these communities.

NOTES

1. McKim Marriott, "Caste Ranking and Food Transactions: A Matrix Analysis," in *Structure and Change in Indian Society*, eds. Milton Singer and Bernard Cohn (Chicago: Aldine Publishing Company, 1968), pp. 133–171.

Gerald D. Berreman, "The Study of the Caste Ranking in India," *South Western Journal of Anthropology* 21 (1965): 120–121.

Edward B. Harper, "Social Consequences of an 'Unsuccessful' Low Caste Movement," in *Social Mobility in the Caste System in India*, ed. James Silverberg (The Hague: Mouton, 1968), pp. 64–65.

2. Stanley A. Freed, "Objective Method of Determining the Collective Caste Hierarchy of an Indian Village," *American Anthropologist* 65 (1963): 879–891.

3. Ibid., p. 888.

4. M. N. Srinivas, "The Social System of a Mysore Village," in *Village India: Studies in the Little Community*, ed. McKim Marriott (Chicago: The University of Chicago Press, 1955), pp. 19–26.

Alan R. Beals, "Interplay Among Factors of Change in a Mysore Village," in *Village India*, ed. Marriott, p. 88.

Dagfin Sivertsen, *When Caste Barriers Fall: A Study of Social and Economic Changes in a South Indian Village* (New York: Humanities Press, 1963), pp. 30–31.

Andre Beteille, *Caste, Class and Power: Changing Patterns of Stratification in a Tanjor Village* (Berkeley: University of California Press, 1965), pp. 93-94.

Adrian C. Mayer, *Caste and Kinship in Central India: A Village and Its Region* (Berkeley: University of California Press, 1960), p. 33.

McKim Marriott, "Social Structure and Change in a U.P. Village," in *India's Villages*, ed. M. N. Srinivas, (Bombay: Asia Publishing House, 1955), pp. 112–113.

5. Hans H. Gerth and C. Wright Mills, *From Max Weber: Essays in Sociology* (New York: Oxford University Press, 1958), pp. 396–397.

M. N. Srinivas, *Caste in Modern India and Other Essays* (Bombay: Asia Publishing House, 1962), p. 88.

Alan R. Beals, *Gopalpur: A South Indian Village* (New York: Holt, Rinehart and Winston, 1962), pp. 36–37.

Philip Mason, "Unity and Diversity: An Introductory Review," in *India and Ceylon: Unity and Diversity*, ed. Philip Mason (London: Oxford Unitersity Press, 1967), p. 5.

Beteille, *Caste, Class and Power*, p. 15.

Mayer, *Caste and Kinship in Central India*, p. 35.

A. P. Barnabas and Subhash C. Mehta, *Caste in Changing India* (New Delhi: The Indian Institute of Public Administration, 1965), pp. 23–24.

6. Arthur L. Stinchcombe, "The Structure of Stratification Systems," in *International Encyclopedia of the Social Sciences*, ed. David L. Sills (New York: The Macmillan Company and The Free Press, 1968), Vol. 15, pp. 324–332.

David G. Mandelbaum, *Society in India: Continuity and Change* (Berkeley: University of California Press, 1970), Vol. 1, pp. 208–209.

7. S. C. Dube, *Indian Village* (Ithaca: Cornell University Press, 1955), pp. 74–76. Sivertsen, *When Caste Barriers Fall*, p. 54.

8. B. Krishnan, "Social Prestige of Occupations," *Journal of Vocational and Educational Guidance* 3 (1956): 18–22.

Victor S. D'Souza, "Social Grading of Occupations in India," *The Sociological Review* 10 (1962): 145–159; "Social Grading of Village Occupations," *Journal of Gujarat Research Society* 26 (1964): 33–34.

Edwin D. Driver, "Caste and Occupational Structure in Central India," *Social Forces* 41 (1962) 26–31.

David R. Cook, "Prestige of Occupations in India," *Psychological Studies* 7 (1962): 31–37.

9. Doctor, engineer, administrative officer, military officer, lawyer, politician, businessman, primary school teacher, shopkeeper, clerk, military soldier, driver, postman, policeman, skilled worker, unskilled non-agricultural laborer, farmer (owner-operator), agricultural laborer.

10. National Institute of Community Development, *Diffusion of Innovations in Rural Societies-India Phase II Codes* (Hyderabad, India: National Institute of Community of Development, 1968). This project was sponsored jointly by the National Institute of Community Development, Hyderabad, India, and The Michigan State University. The data for the two phase study were gathered during 1966–67 from 108 villages in Andhra Pradesh, Maharashtra and West Bengal. Business, professional and government officer were at the top and cultivator, agricultural operator and agricultural laborer at the bottom of the occupational prestige hierarchy.

11. See Appendix B for the original occupational tables.

Part Four

Changes in The Stratification System

The attempt to understand the changes in the stratification systems of the Indian villages that have been studied must begin with a review of their stratification in the traditional caste system. Using the traditional caste system as a basis to grasp the extent of changes, the important social and structural changes that have taken place since independence in these villages can be described. Emerging patterns in the stratification systems can be noted from the intercorrelations among several stratification variables over three generations. Intergenerational educational and occupational mobility demonstrated the dynamics of the emerging stratification system. Mobility among community influentials indicates the fluidity of the class system. All these elements together will show how the status system is evolving and what its major characteristics are.

CASTE INEQUALITY

Ritual distinctions between castes were widely recognized during the period 1930–46. They greatly influenced the patterns of social relations. Housing patterns in the villages followed caste lines in such a way that higher castes occupied the center of the village, middle castes were located beyond the higher castes at some distance, while the lower castes were concentrated on the periphery in small clusters. These housing arrangements influenced patterns of interaction among the people of the different castes. Castes living in close proximity naturally interacted more than castes living farther apart. Physical facilities (such as wells) in the high-caste neighborhood were not accessible to lower castes. Different sides of village ponds were allocated to the lower castes. Low-caste people refrained from passing by the high-caste homes to avoid the ridicule and reprimands that might come from people fearing pollution from physical contact with them. The castes in the middle range normally waited to use facilities of any sort until after the higher castes had finished using them.

There was a primary school located in Jaiti which was supposed to serve the needs of both Ratu and Bhagu. The children from the lower castes were discouraged by high-caste teachers and the high caste inhabitants of Jaiti, but most middle-range castes were tolerated in the school. Some of the lower-caste children of the villages went to other neighboring villages, where higher castes had less control over the functioning of the schools.

Such menial and lowly occupations as carrying dead cattle out of the village, collecting dung to be sprinkled on the fields for fertilizer, plowing the fields, carrying the palanquin, and serving as village musicians and washermen were performed by the lower castes and exhibited low ritual and occupational status. The practices of eating pork and feast-leftovers and not wearing anything below one's knees, and of standing at a distance in a humble fashion while talking to high-caste persons were common among the lower castes. Therefore, factors such as housing patterns, limitations on the use of physical facilities, practice of traditional occupations, modes of dress, and even physical posture in intercaste interactions were important in the functioning of ritual hierarchy. The nature of traditional occupations and commensal rules were the most important indicators of relative ritual status in this area.

During 1930–46, Jaiti had strict ritual distinctions. The opinions and behaviors of the Brahmins of Jaiti and Ratu defined the ritual status of the different castes. There were no Brahmins in Bhagu, at any time, but close contacts with Ratu and Jaiti and the influence of its only absentee Brahmin zamindar served as points of reference for caste ranking. The ties between Jaiti and Bhagu were very close. In fact, Bhagu's two political factions were aligned with the two prominent Brahmin factions of Jaiti.

The Brahmins in Jaiti and Ratu did not eat with Kshatriyas, but they expected courtesy and ritual respect from them. There were castes in the middle and at the lower levels whose relative ritual rankings changed from context to context; but Kshatriyas cooperated with Brahmins in maintaining such elaborate ritual distinctions.

Violators of caste taboos were punished; the severity of the penalty depended upon the nature of the violation and the status of the violator. Penalties ranged from exclusion from previous privileges of interdining and social intercourse to economic boycott and eviction from the village. Lower castes were subject to more severe penalties than higher castes for the same offense.

Caste rules were more rigid in Jaiti than they were in either Ratu or Bhagu. In Ratu, caste rules were flexible in general interaction but strict on ceremonial occasions. Residential segregation and restrictions on the use of physical facilities in this village were less rigid than in Jaiti. In Bhagu, a predominantly low-caste village, ritual distinctions between castes were even less severe than in Ratu. The rules of interdining were less strict, and very little residential segregation and separation in the use of physical facilities was found. To be sure, on ceremonial occasions various castes followed certain ritual distinctions, but not as elaborately as in Ratu or Jaiti.

The caste councils during this period were strong in all the villages. They controlled the behavior of their members in intercaste relations. Problems related to marriage and divorce were the main areas of their concern. Generally, other caste leaders did not intervene in intracaste matters until one of the parties in the dispute challenged the impartiality of the caste council or decided to take the matter to the police or law courts. During 1930–46, each caste occupied a unique place in the hierarchy of castes, and the degree of rigidity in the caste rules varied from village to village depending on the caste structure and the relative numerical strength of castes in the village.

CHANGES IN CASTE INEQUALITY

It was indicated in Part III that several castes had similar ritual statuses during 1947–65; their ritual statuses were somewhat less differentiated than they were in 1930–46. There were fewer feasts in each of the villages and when they were held, there was less village-wide participation. The participation of lower castes in higher-caste ceremonies declined, since such factors as the loss of income from land resulted in the inability of higher-caste families to meet the big expenses of the village-wide feast. The result was a reduction in the importance of ceremonies in acquiring prestige. Many of the new lower-caste landowners were reluctant to participate according to old conventions by which they were conspicuously degraded. Specialized caste families — priests, potters, barbers, washermen, etc. — who now owned land, demanded more remuneration and gifts for performing their traditional services. Initially, they used subtle ways to avoid confronting higher-caste persons with the issue of changing social relationships — responding to requests for their services with, "I am too busy, come some other time," to communicate that they were no longer available under the traditional arrangements.

When zamindari was abolished, the specialized castes were granted legal ownership of land which they had received as conditional gifts from their clients. The clients recognized that the traditional relations could no longer be maintained and accordingly became less demanding.

Intercaste dining patterns also changed. Many families began to invite only their close kin and a few family friends for feasts and entertained others by serving such things as sweets and tea, which did not require strict observances of commensal rules. These new patterns reduced intercaste participation in ceremonial occasions.

The status differences indicated by the residential patterns, use of public facilities, mode of dress, and forms of intercaste greetings also underwent some changes. Most people wore what they could afford and cared less about the approval of others. Children who went to school or those who worked outside the village could no longer be differentiated as to caste on the basis of dress or forms of greetings. A few persons still felt uncomfortable about not following the old conventions, but their number was dwindling. The changes in the traditional patterns of social relations created situations in which people of different social backgrounds avoided interaction. While anyone could now use any of the village wells and streets, the lower castes built their own wells and carved out new little paths to avoid unpleasant confrontations with the upper castes.

Rejection of ritual caste distinctions increased in all three villages. People began to question social inequality not only in their own villages but elsewhere as well, as the following incident illustrates. Near the end of 1963, two lower-caste leaders of Bhagu went to Jaiti to borrow a few things to be used in a marriage. Since they did not have their own primary school, Bhagu children attended school in Jaiti. The leaders decided to visit the school and see how the children were doing. The school teacher asked them to be seated. Being of a lower caste, they hesitated, but on the insistence of the teacher one of them sat down on a chair. After they had left the school and were on their way home they were met by two high-caste but uneducated young men. The latter said that one of them had violated a traditional caste rule by sitting on the chair in the presence of high-caste teachers and children and therefore needed to be punished. Fearing physical violence, the low-caste men apologized for their action. A few days later these men came to Jaiti and lodged a protest with the higher-caste leaders. The latter did not take the complaint seriously and suggested that intercaste conventions should not be broken. The two men from Bhagu returned to their village and called a meeting of the panchayat. It was unanimously decided that a formal complaint should be filed against the two Jaiti men and the high-caste leaders, charging them with caste discrimination in public places. The complaint was sent to the appropriate authorities through the area post office which is located in Jaiti. By the end of 1965 they had received no reply, however. They suspected that the postmaster (from a middle-range caste) of Jaiti did not send the letter due to the pressure of the Jaiti village leaders.

There were many more incidents in these villages in which the superior status of higher castes was challenged by lower castes. Several times upper-caste men — including the son of the Brahmin head of the village panchayat of Jaiti — were insulted and beaten by lower-caste people. In reprisal for the Jaiti incident, however, upper-caste persons forced several members of low-caste families to leave the village of Jaiti temporarily. Similar incidents had occurred in Ratu. When confrontation became serious and upper or middle-range castes used their caste superiority as a weapon, they were challenged. Such confrontations have become quite common in Jaiti and Ratu in recent years.

In Bhagu, members of the higher castes began to consider greater equality with the lower castes earlier than in the other villages. An interesting event which took place within Bhagu involved an upper-caste man who kept a lower-caste woman as a mistress — she lived with him in a part of his house. He was excommunicated by his caste and regarded as an outcaste. In 1961 the woman died. Neither the people of the man's caste nor those of the woman's caste helped the man cremate his mistress. A few years later, when the man died, his former caste fellows were hesitant to arrange his cremation. After some thought they decided to go ahead with all the ceremonies as they were the only close kin of the deceased. Members of the woman's caste also participated in the funeral procession. Such adjustments in intercaste relations would have been impossible during 1930–46, even in the permissive atmosphere of Bhagu, and they are impossible in Jaiti and Ratu even today.

In the beginning of 1955, a relatively rich family from one of the lower castes in Ratu organized a village feast to which some of the middle-range castes were invited. The understanding was, of course, that the lower-caste people would stay away until the higher castes had dined. The food was cooked by Brahmins in clarified butter and the lower-caste host stayed away as promised. Never before had Brahmins done any cooking for a lower caste; nor had any of the families from the upper or middle-range castes ever dined at the house of a lower-caste family previously. Some of the castes held meetings to decide whether or not they should participate in the feast. According to earlier ritual practices, the decision — if one had been required at all — should have been negative, but on this occasion, some middle-range caste members pleaded that the times had changed, that the lower castes were numerically dominant, and that it was better to maintain good relations with them than to continue to adhere to traditional rules. Most people decided not to participate in the feast, but a few castes were split on the issue. Some members of the middle-range castes dined in the feast. Those who participated argued that it was unnecessary to follow rigidly age-old conventions of intercaste relations. They were ridiculed for a few days but no serious sanctions were used against them.

Events like the above happened more often during 1947–65 than during 1930–46, pointing to a decline in the observance of traditional ritual patterns. Many castes claimed equal ritual status to their adjacent castes and did not maintain elaborate ritual distinctions in intercaste relations. Despite a decline in ritual distinctions, castes did not merge themselves with each other.

ECONOMIC AND POLITICAL INEQUALITY

During 1930–46, the zamindari system, in which a few high caste families in each village had greater control of economic and political power prevailed. The zamindars were recognized by the government, and were responsible for paying the land revenue on the land titled in their names. Typically, zamindars living in these villages cultivated part of their landholdings with hired labor and rented the rest to the tenants. The majority of tenants were from the lower and middle-range castes. There were many higher-caste families that owned very little land, but neither they nor the village-based zamindars were willing to enter into zamindar-tenant relationships. Higher-caste families were often tenants for absentee zamindars. They had more freedom and there were fewer occasions upon which they were reminded of their dependent status than were the lower-caste families.

There are two ways that the degree of inequality in the distribution of land can be assessed: one, by examining the legal ownership, the other by observing the actual use of the land. On the basis of legal ownership, Bhagu showed the greatest inequality, with one zamindar owning approximately 80 percent of the land. Next came Ratu, and Jaiti was last with the lowest concentration. But this picture of concentration of land based upon the legal ownership alone would prove unrealistic, since during this period the privilege of using land was a better indicator of property status than legal ownership.

The zamindars legally controlled substantial amounts of land in each village. This land was rented to tenants, many of whom had occupied the same piece of land for generations. It was this latter kind of land distribution more than legal ownership that indicated a family's property status. Most tenants stayed on the land they had rented and were made owners after the abolition of zamindari. Thus, the legal ownership of the land changed, but this change did not greatly affect the distribution of the families who actually cultivated it.

It was indicated in Part III that zamindars had considerable political power in their villages. Their tenants consulted them in various kinds of matters and followed their commands. The heads of traditional village panchayats in the three villages were Kshatriyas and Brahmins. The traditional village head in Bhagu was a Kshatriya, but he had very little influence in village affairs because a parallel position was created by the powerful zamindar of the village and was filled by a lower-caste person. The traditional village head was appointed on the recommendation of the divisional administrative officer, in consultation with the police and other important people in the village. Generally, a strong man was appointed who could maintain law and order in the village and had good relations with the police and with revenue officials. A village head continued in office until his death; generally the position was passed on to one of his sons or a close kinsman if he was considered capable of shouldering the responsibility. The other leaders belonged to high dominant castes and held large landholdings. They settled minor disputes and helped the village head maintain law and order. They used poor and disadvantaged groups in such community projects as building and repairing village schools, lanes, and drains and cleaning wells and ponds. The people who maintained these facilities benefited least from them.

The office of the traditional village head constituted the highest political power in the village. People had to get village problems settled through him. Frequently he withheld information to show his power. Government officials and other outsiders conducted their business through the traditional village head. He discouraged direct communication between the village people and officials. The key to his power lay in the secrecy with which he conducted business with outsiders. People were always afraid that he would implicate them in some complicated legal matter if they did not maintain cordial relations with him. This fear was greater among the lower castes and the poor people.

The degree of support from the officials in the area depended upon the efficiency of the head of the panchayat in maintaining law and order; they generally did not care what means he used to achieve this goal. The official evaluations of the head of the panchayat rested in the report of the petty government officials who extracted money and other favors through him.

Lower-caste groups were under great pressure to follow the decisions of the local leaders; even in the event of outright injustice police and divisional officials were not of much help. When the high castes rejected decisions of the head, government officials and other leaders from neighboring villages often intervened to avoid major local confrontations between parties of comparable social and economic ranks. The lower castes neither mediated in disputes nor were allowed to hear higher-caste disputants, even if the discussions were carried out in a public place. The middle-range castes were allowed to be present, but they were rarely called upon to mediate in the higher-caste disputes.

The zamindars, the village head and a few other leaders controlled the political life of the village. The leaders in Jaiti were very arbitrary in making most decisions. If disputes involved persons of different caste statuses the decisions were generally made in favor of the higher castes. In fact, it was considered rude for a lower-caste man to stand up against a higher-caste man. Most of the time the complaints of lower-caste persons were not heard at all. In Ratu because there were only two higher-caste families and some families from the middle and lower castes who had begun to get rich, the village leaders were less arbitrary in dispensing justice. In Jaiti the police were more frequently used against those who did not comply with the decisions. In Ratu the police came less frequently, and in Bhagu they appeared least of all. Irrespective of the numbers of leaders involved, Bhagu was more democratic than Ratu. In terms of political inequality, Jaiti was highest and was followed by Ratu and Bhagu.

CHANGES IN ECONOMIC STATUS AND POWER

Table IV–I indicated that while the average landholding of families was very close for each of the three villages, a degree of inequality did exist among them. Differences in the size of standard deviations indicated that this was true. Ratu had greater economic inequality than Jaiti or Bhagu during both periods. Jaiti in turn, had greater economic inequality than Bhagu. The lesser degree of economic inequality in Bhagu was due to the absentee zamindar and his impartial treatment of all his lower-caste tenants. The landholding of families did not change much over time, but there were certain conditions that increased the inequality during 1947–65. Community Development programs were organized in such a way that they provided more credit facilities to buy improved seeds, fertilizers, and agricultural implements to those who owned larger amounts of land. The programs provided little for the landless or the smaller landholders. In this way, big farmers were better able to introduce improved seeds and fertilizers and thus increased their productivity, creating greater economic disparity during 1947–65 than existed in 1930–46.

The establishment of statutory village panchayats, elected on the basis of adult franchise, changed the political structure of the villages by adding new leadership positions and making the traditional power structure defunct. The establishment of cooperative societies provided a few more leadership positions.

Case studies of three panchayat elections during 1947–65 showed that panchayat leaders were recruited from quite heterogeneous backgrounds. Deliberate efforts were apparently made to achieve proportional representation of each caste in the village leadership positions, but such efforts were more vigorously pursued in Bhagu and Ratu than in Jaiti.

In Bhagu the important and elderly people tried to maximize representation in the panchayat of each faction and locality. The only

Table IV-1

DISTRIBUTION OF INEQUALITY IN THE THREE STRATIFICATION VARIABLES IN THE THREE VILLAGES (IN TERMS OF STANDARD DEVIATIONS)*

Stratification Variables	Jaiti			Ratu			Bhagu		
	FR	R	S	FR	R	S	FR	R	S
Land	4.63	4.61	5.16	5.81	5.54	4.12	3.24	3.15	3.93
	(4.65)	(4.66)	(6.21)	(4.73)	(4.49)	(4.54)	(4.53)	(4.48)	(6.00)
Education	.50	.70	.92	.39	.75	1.15	.28	.49	.82
	(.23)	(.46)	(.67)	(.14)	(.49)	(.77)	(.08)	(.17)	(.72)
Occupation	1.19	1.08	1.88	.98	1.08	1.95	.00	.64	.87
	(2.32)	(2.25)	(3.15)	(2.34)	(2.40)	(3.00)	(2.00)	(2.05)	(2.08)

*The means for corresponding standard deviations are given in the parentheses.
FR = Fathers of respondents
R = Respondents
S = Sons of respondents

political position for which bitter election fights ensued was that of the head of the village panchayat. Such factions also existed in Jaiti and Ratu, but none of them were based upon a single caste. In Jaiti the important leaders of factions were high-caste persons. In Ratu the faction leadership was mixed, and in Bhagu this leadership was entirely low-caste. The factional alliances were not permanent; they shifted on the basis of economic and political interests.

In Jaiti, the elections for head of the village panchayat were contested by higher-caste candidates. They used persuasion, intimidation, and physical violence as means of persuading the lower castes to support one side or the other. In Ratu, the candidates were from the middle-range and lower-castes. The upper castes and a few important families from the numerically dominant middle-range castes influenced the choice of candidates. The selections of candidates were not made on the basis of leadership qualities, but simply on the considerations of victory. Since the upper castes were very few in number, they were not sure of getting elected and refrained from contesting the election. The first head of the panchayat in Ratu was a lower-caste man; in two subsequent terms a politically ineffective man from one of the middle-range castes was elected. In Bhagu all the three heads of the village panchayat were lower-caste persons and were elected unanimously.

In contrast to the position of head of the village panchayat, the position of member of the village panchayat was less important. The members did not play constructive roles without the support of the head of the panchayat. There were fewer volunteers to run for office than there were positions available. Such situations were more common in Ratu and Bhagu than in Jaiti. In Jaiti the factional bitterness was always present, and each faction persuaded some of its followers to offer themselves for political offices. In the third election, for instance, there were contests for the membership of the panchayat in this village. Anyone running for office in the panchayat had to have cleared all his panchayat tax. Since many people were unwilling or too poor to pay, they were disqualified from running for an office. A small fee also had to be paid by the candidates to obtain permits to run in the election. Most people saw no immediate payoff for holding an office in the panchayat. Some faction leaders arranged money to fund candidates so that they could influence the functioning of the panchayat. In Jaiti and Ratu, lower-caste leaders were patronized by the opposing factions. In Bhagu several positions remained vacant in all three terms of the panchayat due to politics of compromise.

We referred earlier to two other organizations, namely the nyay panchayat (judicial council) and the cooperative society. The former was created for a group of ten to fifteen villages to dispense justice in minor village disputes. It was a judicial body and its decisions were binding upon the parties, unless appealed in the higher courts or vetoed by the divisional officials of the region. It was made up of representatives from each village panchayat under its jurisdiction So far, the heads of the nyay panchayat have been persons of higher castes. A wealthy Brahmin from Ratu was elected its chairman in 1961. All the three villages fell in the same nyay panchayat circle. Between 1949–51 a Brahmin and a Kshatriya from other villages were elected to the chairmanship, both of whom were wealthy in the area and had greater access to political parties and politicians at the district and state level.

The two cooperative societies, one for Jaiti and Bhagu, and the other for Ratu and a few other villages were created to meet the credit needs of the village people. These cooperatives were mostly financed and supervised by the government. The villagers were shareholders, and they were entitled to elect a chairman for each cooperative. The two cooperatives came into being in 1952 and the same chairmen of both of them have continued in office until the present. Normally a chairman was supposed to be relatively wealthy, literate, and experienced in money matters. The government officials who supervised these cooperatives played an important role in the election of the chairman. Besides the chairman for each cooperative, five to seven members were either elected or appointed. The leadership of the cooperative societies in Jaiti and Ratu was in the hands of upper and middle-range castes. One or two members from the lower castes were coopted.

The new political institutions increased the number of leaders in each village. The panchayat, which was the most important political institution, was not controlled exclusively by the higher castes. The numerically dominant lower castes bargained with higher castes and were represented in these local bodies. Factionalism increased and important leaders challenged each other in various matters right after each election. They also confronted opposition from those who were not leaders.

In 1964, the head of the village panchayat in Jaiti decided that the new village street would pass through a piece of land owned by a lower-caste family. It was alleged that he did not consult other members of the panchayat in making the decision because he wanted to take revenge on this stubborn lower-caste family by destroying the only piece of land it owned. There was a confrontation and the family refused to let the street go through its land without any compensation. The leaders of other factions supported the lower-caste family and encouraged the confrontation. In desperation, the head of the village panchayat filed a court case alleging that the lower-caste family stopped the construction of the village street against the wishes of the village panchayat. The matter was left undecided because a majority of the members of the panchayat avoided taking sides. The

moral support was stronger towards the lower-caste family as the inten-
tions of the head of the panchayat were only partly guided by the
"public good."

In another incident, the head of the Jaiti panchayat could not complete the construction of a school for girls because he chose a site near
his house without seeking the consent of the village people. Originally
the school was supposed to be located in the center of the village.
People refused to contribute labor. Other leaders of the village
panchayat did not allow him to spend any money from the panchayat
funds. The government aid allocated for the school was spent in
erecting half of the building in 1963; no additional work was done
until 1966. However, the entire village cooperated in renovating the
old school. Interestingly, the head of the village panchayat did not
play any role in the renovation project.

The ruling faction of Ratu distributed unclaimed land to its supporters but did not give any land to a few others who were also landless. A case was filed in the court in 1963 by the landless people alleging that some village leaders unlawfully and deliberately did not
recognize their claims in the village property. These leaders yielded
and some of the land was redistributed to adjust the claims of these
people, but the case was still continuing in the court at the end of
this study. Such alleged injustice affected the efficiency of the leaders.

The panchayat leaders of Ratu decided to build a school in the
village in 1962. Part of the funds were to come from the Community
Development Block and the rest of the resources were to be raised by
the village itself. Due to alleged partiality in the distribution of land,
the panchayat leaders did not gain the support of the entire village
and the school could not be built.

In contrast to Jaiti and Ratu, Bhagu had the full support of the
people in the projects designed to improve wells, village lanes, ponds,
etc. The two factions checked each other to see that neither did anything that could hurt the interest of the people. Factional bitterness was low and did not interfere with the normal functioning of
village life. The leaders held their meetings in public places and
all were invited to attend and speak. Attempts were made to achieve
consensus in arriving at a decision. The political life of this village
could be described as the politics of compromise in contrast to the
divisive atmosphere of Jaiti and Ratu.

Events such as described indicated that during 1947–65, these villages developed a new political culture in which people of heterogeneous backgrounds played leadership roles. The political life of these
villages was no longer controlled by a handful of families. The leaders
did not go unchallenged if they overstepped their boundaries. Therefore, there was less political inequality during 1947–65 than during
1930–46. The nonleader families entered into leadership positions with

greater ease during 1947–65. Bhagu showed the least political inequality and the greatest ease of access to leadership positions; next
came Ratu; and last came Jaiti, in which it was more difficult for
lower-caste persons to get into leadership positions or to expect justice from predominantly higher-caste leaders.

EDUCATIONAL AND OCCUPATIONAL INEQUALITY

Access to education was limited during 1930–46. The lower-caste
poor were discouraged from acquiring any education. More than 70
percent of the people in each village were illiterate, with only a few
percentage points difference between villages. When the villages were
compared for inequality for the period 1930–46 (See Table IV–I),
Jaiti was found to have the greatest educational inequality, Ratu to
have an intermediate amount, and Bhagu the least. Education was
more a mark of high status than a means to pursue nonagricultural
occupations during this period.

A few Brahambhatt and Teli families of Ratu and Ahir families of
Jaiti worked in urban and industrial centers; within a few years
they were able to increase the size of their landholdings. Typically
those families that participated in urban and industrial occupations
were predominantly from the middle-range castes with smaller landholdings. According to Table IV–1, Jaiti had greater occupational
inequality than either Ratu or Bhagu. In Bhagu, all the villagers
claimed that they pursued agricultural occupations, so that any existing occupational inequality was within that category.

CHANGES IN EDUCATIONAL AND OCCUPATIONAL INEQUALITY

The mean level of education increased greatly over the generations
in the three villages (See Table IV-1). Differences in educational level
between the villages narrowed in the second generation, and narrowed even further in the third. With the increase in educational opportunities, differences in the amount of education became increasingly important to caste members in subsequent generations.

The increases in the amount of education from 1930 to 1965 were
due in part to the presence of more educational facilities and in part
to a greater willingness of the whole community to admit castes
which had usually been excluded from school in the past. Also, increased contact with urban environments during 1947–65 enabled
people to see the advantages of education, thus motivating them to
attend school.

Inequalities in education increased over time in each village, but
such increases were greater in Bhagu than in Jaiti or Ratu. Among
the three villages during 1947–65, the degree of educational inequality
was most pronounced in Ratu, moderate in Jaiti, and least in Bhagu.

Educational inequality was positively related to the mean amount of education in each village. The people of Bhagu had little education generally and thus showed little inequality in education. The mean level of education in Jaiti was higher because a few people were relatively well educated, causing greater educational inequality.

The positive association between mean amount of education and degree of educational inequality in the villages persisted through time. Each village's relative position with regard to educational inequality continued into the third generation — the sons of the respondents. Between 1930–46 and 1947–65 participation in nonagricultural occupations increased in Bhagu and Ratu, but declined slightly in Jaiti. The comparison of means of occupational rankings over three generations in Jaiti and Ratu indicated that in the third generation there was a considerable increase in the numbers participating in nonagricultural occupations. In Bhagu, however, the third generation showed only a slight increase in participation in these occupations.

Table IV–1 indicates that there were no great changes in the degree of occupational inequality in any village until the third generation. Compared to Jaiti or Ratu, Bhagu had the least diversified occupational structure and the lowest occupational inequality throughout the period studied.

It can be suggested that in 1930–46 caste status, size of landholdings and level of education showed a higher degree of interdependence than level of education and occupational status. In Bhagu for instance, the lower degree of interdependence was obviously due to the fact that it was a predominantly lower-caste village in which lower-caste families held most of the land, and to the fact that occupational status was invariant. The leadership was held by a few families on a hereditary basis. These families belonged to higher castes and had greater landholdings and some education, but they did not participate in nonagricultural occupations.

The greatest degree of congruence between caste status, property status, and political power in the three villages was in the zamindar group. The zamindari system made caste status the most important factor in the political stratification system since access to leadership positions and ownership of land were both largely limited to higher-caste persons. Therefore, education and occupation were not highly associated with each other during 1930–46. Education was moderately correlated with the other variables, but occupation had a very low association with each of them. The higher association between caste status, legal ownership of land, and political power is logical in an ascriptive type of stratification system. It can be stated with certainty that a handful of families in each village occupied the apex of the stratification system. Much depended on the position of a family in the local ritual, economic and political structures; these statuses were transferred from one generation to the next on a hereditary basis.

Even though these Indian villages furnished highly congruous caste and class models, they were still far from being a pure caste model of stratification because the populations in these villages had differential access to the various sources of status. For instance, the majority of higher-caste families were not wealthy and many from the middle-range castes and a few from lower castes were even better off than the former. There was a higher degree of congruence on various status dimensions among the community influentials, while others were less concerned about their discrepant statuses.

The abolition of zamindari and establishment of statutory local bodies created a new atmosphere that affected the nature of equality. Zamindari was abolished in 1951–52 in these villages. The burden of collection of land revenue shifted from zamindars to the state government. Tenants were for the first time given the opportunity to acquire full ownership of the land they tilled. The impact of the abolition of zamindari, as mentioned earlier, was keenly felt by the big zamindars because they incurred greater economic and political losses compared to their smaller counterparts who cultivated most of their land themselves. In these villages, the absentee zamindars lost almost all of their land to their tenants and succeeded in selling only a small proportion of it. The local zamindars only partly succeeded in dislodging their tenants, which meant that people were freed from their traditional bondage and could act more independently. Waste land and unoccupied land were declared the property of the entire village, and the landless and the poor were supposed to benefit from them.

It has already been pointed out that the political power of the zamindars and other influentials was jeopardized by the establishment of new panchayats in 1949. The abolition of zamindari and the establishment of the new panchayats began to disturb the great convergence of caste status, property status and political power among the landlords and influential families. The representation of lower castes in the village panchayats marked a new era of political relations. The numerical strength of the lower castes attracted politically ambitious higher-caste families to develop alliances based upon mutual interests.

The new panchayats had greater power. They were entrusted with the responsibility of planning and carrying out civic projects, levying taxes in the village, and distributing unclaimed land to the landless and the poor. Lack of education did not hinder participation in the new organization; an official at the village level was available to assist in the secretarial work and the maintenance of panchayat records. These villages did not respond to the abolition of zamindari and

the establishment of the new panchayats in a uniform manner. Their
histories and social structural peculiarities provided some continuities
and influenced the distribution of resources in different patterns.

THE INTERGENERATIONAL ANALYSIS

Since the data were collected from all families in the villages, the
generational findings reflect the stratification systems of their respective time periods. Fathers of respondents represent 1930–46, while
respondents themselves reflect the period 1947–65, and sons of respondents reveal emerging future patterns. Tables IV–2, IV–5 and
IV-8 display the intercorrelations among the stratification variables
for the generation of fathers of respondents. In Jaiti and Ratu, caste
status, size of landholding and level of education had medium and
higher correlations.[1] The correlation of occupational status with other
stratification variables was lower in comparison to other correlations.
Except for the correlation of level of education with caste status
and occupational status, the remaining correlations were higher in
Ratu when compared with those of Jaiti.

The difference in the correlation of size of landholding with caste
status and occupational status needs some explanation. Members of
numerically larger middle-range castes did not mind working in
urban and industrial occupations even when they owned land in the
village. The higher castes generally avoided manual labor in either
agricultural or nonagricultural occupations, even if they were relatively poor, because it would have been demeaning to their ritual
rank. Jaiti had fewer enterprising middle-range caste people than
Ratu and they could not change occupations as freely as their counterparts in Ratu due to the greater higher-caste dominance that persisted in Jaiti.

In Bhagu, only size of landholding and level of education were
correlated, while other correlations were close to zero. This was
mainly due to its being a predominantly low-caste village, and to its
marked lack of occupational differentiation.

It was noted that within the higher castes, those individuals who
were high on other stratification variables enjoyed higher general
status compared to their caste fellows. Lower-caste persons who
ranked high on other stratification variables were accorded higher
general status than other people of similar caste ranks, but even so
they were treated with contempt by less fortunate upper-caste people.
Often the more educated and affluent acted as spokesmen of their respective castes and were the first to be consulted by others on matters
affecting members of their castes.

The low correlations between stratification variables indicated that
the stratification system was more flexible than one might have ex-

TABLES IV–2, IV–3, IV–4

INTERCORRELATIONS AMONG STRATIFICATION VARIABLES ACROSS THREE GENERATIONS IN JAITI

	Fathers of Respondents IV-2				Respondents IV-3				Sons of Respondents IV-4			
	1	2	3	4	1	2	3	4	1	2	3	4
1. Caste*	—	.31	.48	.19	—	.32	.53	.29	—	.38	.78	.63
2. Land		—	.33	.04		—	.28	-.14		—	.36	.11
3. Education**			—	.24			—	.20			—	.69
4. Occupation***				—				—				—
Number of Cases	209	209	209	209	224	224	224	224	52	52	52	52

*Eighteen-point caste ranking scale used for fathers of respondents and five-point caste ranking scale for respondents and sons.

**Fifth grade and below = 1, 6th to 9th grade = 2, 10th grade and above = 3.

***Agricultural labor = 1, farmer = 2, unskilled nonagriculture labor = 3, skilled worker = 4, service = 5, clerical = 6, primary school teacher = 7, business and professional = 8.

TABLES IV-5, IV-6, IV-7

INTERCORRELATIONS AMONG STRATIFICATION VARIABLES ACROSS THREE GENERATIONS IN RATU

	Fathers of Respondents IV-5				Respondents IV-6				Sons of Respondents IV-7			
	1	2	3	4	1	2	3	4	1	2	3	4
1. Caste*	—	.64	.40	.29	—	.63	.38	.09	—	.57	.78	.78
2. Land		—	.35	.21		—	.36	-.03		—	.54	.59
3. Education**			—	.15			—	.16			—	.72
4. Occupation***				—				—				—
Number of Cases	64	64	63	63	71	71	71	71	22	22	22	22

*Eighteen-point caste ranking scale used for fathers of respondents and five-point caste ranking scale for respondents and sons.

**Fifth grade and below = 1, 6th to 9th grade = 2, 10th grade and above = 3.

***Agricultural labor = 1, Farmer = 2, unskilled nonagriculture labor = 3, skilled worker = 4, service = 5, clerical = 6, primary school teacher = 7, business and professional = 8.

TABLES IV-8, IV-9, IV-10

INTERCORRELATIONS AMONG STRATIFICATION VARIABLES ACROSS THREE GENERATIONS IN BHAGU

	Fathers of Respondents IV-8				Respondents IV-9				Sons of Respondents IV-10			
	1	2	3	4	1	2	3	4	1	2	3	4
1. Caste*	—	.07	.01	.00	—	.08	-.02	-.15	—	-.39	-.21	-.01
2. Land		—	.36	.00		—	.04	-.13		—	.51	.19
3. Education**			—	.00			—	.11			—	-.14
4. Occupation***				—				—				—
Number of Cases	67	66	67	67	84	83	84	84	18	17	18	18

*Eighteen-point caste ranking scale used for fathers of respondents and five-point caste ranking scale for respondents and sons.

**Fifth grade and below = 1, 6th to 9th grade = 2, 10th grade and above = 3.

***Agricultural labor = 1, farmer = 2, unskilled nonagriculture labor = 3, skilled worker = 4, service = 5, clerical = 6, primary school teacher = 7, business and professional = 8.

pected during 1930–46. If we consider these findings in conjunction with the two-class system that prevailed during this period, we would conclude that status inconsistency was tolerated for all the community influentials. The maintenance of stratification by community influentials in general kept other higher-caste people from resisting social change more vigorously than they did. Tables IV–3, IV–6 and IV–9 display the correlations of stratification variables for each generation of respondents in the three villages. An inspection of these tables indicates that in Jaiti and Ratu caste status, size of landholding, and level of education had high or medium correlations.

The correlation of caste status with occupational status was higher in Jaiti than in Ratu because in the former there were proportionately more higher-caste people with some education who participated in nonagricultural occupations; in Ratu most participants in nonagricultural occupations came from educated middle-range castes.

The correlation of occupational status with size of landholding was low and negative in all of the three villages. This correlation can be explained by the fact that people who did not have enough land to support their families often found jobs in the nonagricultural sector rather than working on the farms of others. Not all succeeded in finding nonagricultural work due to the limited supply of such jobs.

Correlations between stratification variables in Bhagu were lower than in Jaiti or Ratu. In Bhagu occupational status showed a degree of association with other stratification variables which indicated that more people worked in nonagricultural occupations. The negative correlation between caste status and occupational status in Bhagu was mainly due to an increasing amount of nonagricultural employment in a predominantly lower-caste village. It is interesting to note that education and diversified occupational participation not only increased in this generation, but their relationship was positive, suggesting that they go hand in hand.

On the basis of the correlations between the variables we might conclude that the stratification systems for the respondents' generation were not much different from those of their fathers' generation. But this similarity was greater in Ratu than in Jaiti or Bhagu. In Ratu, only the correlations of occupational status with caste status and with size of landholding decreased in the respondents' generation, while the remaining were stable. In Jaiti, on the other hand, only the correlation between caste status and size of landholding was stable, while the correlations of caste status with level of education and occupational status increased, and the correlations between size of landholding, level of education and occupational status decreased. Overall, Jaiti showed decreasing correlations from the fathers' generation to the respondents' generation.

In Bhagu the correlations of caste status with the size of landholding and level of education were stable because of low caste, small plots, and little education generally; but the correlations between the size of landholding and level of education decreased, showing that enrollment in schools was independent of size of landholding there. Correlations between occupational status and the other stratification variables began to appear in the respondents' generation.

In the overview, Bhagu showed greater association between stratification variables other than caste status in the respondents' generation than the other villages did. It was noted that much of the stability between the two generations came from the correlations of caste status with other stratification variables in Jaiti and Ratu particularly, while the differences in all of the villages were mainly due to changes in the correlations of occupational status with other stratification variables.

The changes in some of the correlations between the two generations needed some explanations. In Jaiti (See Tables IV–2 and IV–3) the correlation of caste status with occupational status is increased from .19 in the fathers' generation to .29 during the respondents' generation. This change was attributed to increased occupational opportunities and motivation on the part of higher castes to take advantage of them. Unlike Jaiti's, Ratu's (see Tables IV–5 and IV–6) correlations between caste status and occupational status declined from .29 in the fathers' generation to .09 in the respondents' generation. This happened because Ratu had proportionately more people in the middle-range caste category than Jaiti, and they participated more actively in nonagricultural occupations than others. The change from a correlation of .04 between size of landholding and occupational status to −.14 in Jaiti, and from .21 to −.03 in Ratu indicated that those who *could* subsist on land did not find it necessary to compete for nonagricultural occupations with people who could not.

In Bhagu expected correlations between occupational status and other stratification variables emerged in the respondents' generation primarily as a result of increased occupational diversity (see Tables IV–8 and IV–9). There was also a dramatic change in the correlation of size of landholding and level of education from .36 for the fathers' generation to .04 for the respondents' generation. Several factors seemed to have influenced this change. During the fathers' generation, the only accessible primary school was located in Jaiti, where lower castes were discouraged from attending the school. A few lower-caste people who had sufficient land sent their children to the nearby city where they lived with relatives and completed a few years of education. But during the respondents' generation, a number of educational facilities became accessible and interference in the education of low-caste children by the higher castes declined. This helped many children from disadvantaged lower-caste families to acquire some education and a few to finish school.

The ascriptive nature of leadership during the generation of fathers of respondents, coupled with the small number of leadership positions open to them during their appropriate age span, made the study of generational change in leadership futile, especially since none of the sons of respondents were leaders. The new leadership in the respondents' generation was open to all in principle, and the number of leadership positions increased with the creation of new local bodies. Intercorrelations of leadership with the other stratification variables for the respondents' generation in the three villages were as follows:

	Jaiti	Ratu	Bhagu
Caste	.27	.23	.11
Land	.46	.43	.44
Education	.22	.04	.25
Occupation	−.06	−.05	−.01

The correlations of the four other stratification variables with leadership status for the respondents' generation indicated that only land was highly correlated in the three villages. The association of leadership with caste depended on the degree of caste differentiation in the village. The proliferation of leadership positions and the new principles of recruitment lessened its association with caste status. There were medium correlations with the level of education, which suggested that education was relevant to the performance of leadership responsibilities. In Ratu the lower correlation with education was due to the fact that most educated persons came from middle-range castes and were engaged in nonagricultural occupations outside the village and had very little time to engage in local politics. In Jaiti and Bhagu the medium correlations between leadership and education need some explanation. In the former, all of the higher caste leaders had some education, and in the latter the politics of compromise put moral pressure on the relatively educated people to help in village affairs. There was no doubt that people in these villages increasingly realized the importance of education in the context of leadership status and there were indications that this association will be even stronger in the future.

The negative associations with occupational status resulted because leaders lived and worked in the village and were engaged in agricultural occupations. Some of the lower-caste leaders even worked as agricultural laborers. The association of leadership status with land and education indicated that there was considerable interdependence between economic power and political power and that education enabled a leader to wield his authority more efficiently. In comparison, the associations of leadership status with other stratification variables during 1947–65 were weaker than during 1930–46, and was clearly due to the emergence of leadership on a nonascriptive basis and the sudden creation of large numbers of leadership positions in the village on the initiative of the state government.

THE STRATIFICATION SYSTEM AND INTERGENERATIONAL CHANGE

The preceeding discussion indicated that the structural characteristics of Bhagu, Ratu, and Jaiti influenced the nature of correlations among the stratification variables. The differences between the intercorrelations of two generations indicated that the respondents' generation was marked by certain institutional changes and the stratification system was still in the process of transition. In other words, the impact of these changes was not fully realized, although on the surface many effects were noticed. The third generation (sons of respondents) had actually been most affected by the recent changes, and the pattern of correlations for this generation indicates the nature of the emerging stratification system.

The intercorrelations among caste status, size of landholding, level of education and occupational status in the third generation were higher compared to the two previous generations of fathers of respondents, and respondents in Jaiti (see Tables IV–2, IV–3, and IV–4) and Ratu (see Tables IV–5, IV–6, and IV–7). In Bhagu there were some average increases in the intercorrelations in the third generation but the correlation between caste status and occupational status — which was −.15 in the second generation — changed to almost no correlation in the third generation (see Tables IV–8, IV–9, and IV–10). Also, the correlation between level of education and occupational status changed from .11 in the respondents' generations to −.14 in the generation of sons of respondents. Once again, the explanation of this shift is that Bhagu was a predominantly lower-caste community and some people in the third generation took advantage of the governmental employment policy of preferential treatment for people who had suffered from social disabilities in the past. Therefore, it was easier for a lower-caste person to get a job with a lower level of education in competition with a higher-caste person with more education. Further, sons still in school or recently out had high educational achievement but had not yet reached their occupational potentials.

A closer examination of Tables IV–4, IV–7, and IV–10 indicated that generally all four stratification variables hang together more tightly in the third generation than in the previous two generations. In Ratu and Jaiti caste status was found to be still an important dimension of social stratification, particularly where the local social structure was more differentiated. In Bhagu, however, caste status remained relatively unimportant. During the sons' generation in Jaiti and Ratu, higher correlations of caste status with the level of education (.78 in both Jaiti and Ratu) and with occupational status (.63 in Jaiti and .78 in Ratu) need some additional explanation (see Tables IV–4 and IV–7). Many would assert that it was not the ritual aspects of caste status per se, but nonritual aspects such as higher economic status and greater contacts with the outside world which contributed to these higher correlations. The ritual elements of caste status are still correlated with its nonritual elements. However, given certain contemporary trends, one might speculate that such a relationship will change in the long run when lower-caste people become more able to enhance their educational and occupational attainments. The vicious circle will be broken by such factors as more education and greater occupational participation, trends which are already observable, which will make greater mobility in the status system possible. This line of reasoning is supported by the higher correlations between level of education and occupational status in the third generation. In the third generation, the correlations in Bhagu were lower compared to those in Jaiti or Ratu, primarily due to its lower caste and increasing occupational differentiation. We have already explained that the correlation of −.14 between the level of education and occupational status in Bhagu was due in part also to protective discrimination for the lower-caste in employment. The nontraditional aspects of stratification were apparently taking root.

People in Indian villages at the time of this study did not have birth certificates and the information on age therefore depended upon the guesses of the respondents, recollections of other members of the families and sometimes memories of the neighbors. In cross-checking, it was found that ages reported for specific fathers of respondents had wide discrepancies. The data on ages of respondents themselves and their sons were more reliable than those of fathers. The insufficient number of sons of respondents and the possibility of nonrandom error in the age of respondents precluded systematic age cohort analysis.

The correlational analysis was replicated after excluding those cases that had respondents above 60 years or below 35 years (see Appendix C, Tables C1–C12). The choice of these age limits rested on the fact that a person who was more than 60 years old would legitimately belong to the generation of fathers of respondents in these communities. The lower age limit was determined on the basis that it was possible for a 35 year old respondent to have a son 18 years old or older. One of the 35 year old respondents had a son who was more than 18 years old, an obvious function of the age of marriage. Generally, the lower age limit for marriage for boys was about 14 years and for girls 12 years in the generation of respondents. These criteria resulted in a loss of 67 cases in Jaiti (30 percent), 28 in Ratu (39 percent) and 33 in Bhagu (39 percent). Our generational distinctions seemed realistic because even after a loss of about 34 percent of the total number of cases, the correlations were reasonably comparable. A few minor fluctuations resulted from insufficient cases, although the general patterns of correlations remained stable across three generations.

EDUCATIONAL AND OCCUPATIONAL MOBILITY

In this research, mobility is studied on educational and occupational dimensions. Caste status was quite stable across generations, although there were fewer caste barriers in 1965 than in the past. The lower castes did not try to emulate the life-styles of the higher castes. They improved their social position through the use of such nontraditional means as votes, or had it improved by government legislation, and sometimes simply by refusal to accept their traditional roles.

The power structure of 1947–65 could not be compared with that of 1930–46. During 1947–65 new village organizations were created on the Indian government's initiative and the number of formal leadership positions was fixed outside the villages. During 1930–46, informal local procedures were used in the recruitment of leaders with the cursory approval of the government officials. The leadership at that time was primarily ascriptive in nature. Sometimes people who owned land in the village but did not live there had considerable political influence in the appointment of local officials. Due to lack of comparability of political procedures between generations, the investigation of leadership mobility was not studied.

The increasing importance of education and occupation in the emerging stratification system made the study of intergenerational educational and occupational mobility especially relevant. There were comparable data on education and occupation over the three generations. Changes in educational and occupational structures between 1930–46 and 1947–65 indicated that there was educational and occupational mobility between the fathers of the respondents and the respondents. Likewise, differences between the respondents and their sons suggested an accentuation of those mobility patterns. In this study, if a father had several sons who lived in different households, the same father provided the status origins for all his sons. Thanks to the less differentiated occupational structure in the fathers' generation and fewer opportunities for career mobility, our data avoided some of the problems of selecting the generation of reference described earlier.

Mobility is defined in this study as the difference between two generations in their level of education or occupation. Since the status attainment scores of the fathers are subtracted from those of their sons, a positive score indicates upward mobility and a negative score downward mobility. Educational and occupational mobility scores are investigated from the fathers to the respondents on the one hand, and from the respondents to their sons on the other.

Educational mobility is conceptualized as a change in the educational level between one generation (a father) and the next (his son). Correlations between educational and occupational status across generations are presented in Tables IV–11, IV–12, and IV–13 for Jaiti, Ratu and Bhagu respectively. The lack of perfect correlations indicates that there was educational mobility between generations. Inspection of these tables indicates that correlations between the sons' education and the respondents' are greater than the correlations between the respondents' and their fathers' except in Bhagu. Mobility tables will help us to understand the amount and nature of changes in educational and occupational status between generations.

Tables IV–14, IV–15, and IV–16 show the amount of educational mobility from fathers to respondents in Jaiti, Ratu, and Bhagu respectively. According to these tables, 35 percent of the respondents in Ratu, 25 percent in Jaiti, and 13 percent in Bhagu were educationally mobile from their fathers' statuses. Only 3 percent in each village were downwardly mobile. The diagonal cells are larger than the cells showing mobility in each educational level, which indicates that there still was a high degree of congruence between the status of respondents and their fathers. These tables also show that those who have moved up or down have travelled only short distances. In terms of upward mobility, the biggest gains came to those respondents whose fathers had no education. It must be pointed out that situated as they were at the very bottom of the social stratification system, any mobility in this group would take the form of upward mobility.

Educational mobility from respondents to their sons is presented in Tables IV–17, IV–18, and IV–19 for Jaiti, Ratu, and Bhagu respectively. Educational mobility for the second generation of respondents to the third generation of sons rose sharply as compared to the mobility from first to second generations in Jaiti and Bhagu. In Ratu, educational mobility declined slightly, although it was still close to Jaiti. Upward mobility far exceeded downward mobility in all three villages, with the greatest upward mobility in Bhagu. Oddly, the amount of downward mobility also increased compared to previous generations of respondents. Unlike previous generations, the sons of the more educated respondents have been more upwardly than downwardly mobile. The mobility of sons of uneducated respondents declined in Ratu and Jaiti, while in Bhagu it increased.

Table IV–11

CORRELATIONS OF EDUCATION AND OCCUPATION ACROSS THREE GENERATIONS
IN JAITI

	1	2	3	4	5	6
1. Education of Fathers of Respondents	—	.52	.51	.24	.11	.41
2. Education of Respondents		—	.67	.20	.20	.52
3. Education of Sons of Respondents			—	.44	.16	.69
4. Occupation of Fathers of Respondents				—	.37	.36
5. Occupation of Respondents					—	.30
6. Occupation of Sons of Respondents						—

Table IV–12

CORRELATIONS OF EDUCATION AND OCCUPATION ACROSS THREE GENERATIONS
IN RATU

	1	2	3	4	5	6
1. Education of Fathers of Respondents	—	.32	.41	.15	.30	.53
2. Education of Respondents		—	.54	.42	.16	.37
3. Education of Sons of Respondents			—	.24	.03	.72
4. Occupation of Fathers of Respondents				—	.29	.46
5. Occupation of Respondents					—	.32
6. Occupation of Sons of Respondents						—

The analysis of mobility tables indicates that generally, educational mobility has increased across generations in all three villages. Upward educational mobility was far greater than downward mobility in each village. Upward mobility appeared in greater magnitude in the third generation of sons of respondents. The diagonal cells have continued to be larger across generations, indicating the fact that the status of origin continued to influence the status of destination. It was noted, however, that the sizes of these cells have proportionately declined, especially those at the higher educational levels, across generations.

Table IV–13

CORRELATIONS OF EDUCATION AND OCCUPATION ACROSS THREE GENERATIONS IN BHAGU

	1	2	3	4	5	6
1. Education of Fathers of Respondents	—	.26	.40	.00	-.04	.11
2. Education of Respondents		—	.21	.00	.11	-.33
3. Education of Sons of Respondents			—	.00	.00	-.14
4. Occupation of Fathers of Respondents				—	.00	.00
5. Occupation of Respondents					—	.00
6. Occupation of Sons of Respondents						—

Table IV–14

EDUCATIONAL MOBILITY FROM FATHERS OF RESPONDENTS TO RESPONDENTS IN JAITI

Education of Fathers	Education of Respondents (in Years)				
	10+	6–9	1–5	None	Total
10th Grade and above	—	—	1	—	1
6th to 9th Grade	—	2	2	1	5
1st to 5th Grade	4	4	26	2	36
None	1	3	35	128	167
Total	5	9	64	131	209

Mobile = 53 (25%)   Upward = 47 (22%)   Downward = 6 (3%)

Table IV–15

EDUCATIONAL MOBILITY FROM FATHERS OF RESPONDENTS TO RESPONDENTS IN RATU

Education of Fathers	Education of Respondents (in Years)				
	10+	6–9	1–5	None	Total
10th Grade and above	—	—	—	—	—
6th to 9th Grade	—	1	—	—	1
1st to 5th Grade	—	2	3	2	7
None	2	2	14	37	55
Total	2	5	17	39	63

Mobile = 22 (35%)   Upward = 20 (32%)   Downward = 2 (3%)

Table IV–16

EDUCATIONAL MOBILITY FROM FATHERS OF RESPONDENTS TO RESPONDENTS IN BHAGU

Education of Fathers	Education of Respondents (in Years)				
	10+	6–9	1–5	None	Total
10th Grade and above	—	—	—	—	—
6th to 9th Grade	—	—	—	—	—
1st to 5th Grade	—	—	4	2	6
None	1	1	5	54	61
Total	1	1	9	56	67

Mobile = 9 (13%)   Upward = 7 (10%)   Downward = 2 (3%)

Table IV–17

EDUCATIONAL MOBILITY FROM RESPONDENTS TO SONS OF RESPONDENTS IN JAITI

Education of Respondents	Education of Sons (in Years)				
	10+	6–9	1–5	None	Total
10th Grade and above	—	—	—	—	—
6th to 9th Grade	1	2	1	—	4
1st to 5th Grade	2	4	6	4	16
None	—	1	5	26	32
Total	3	7	12	30	52

Mobile = 18 (35%)   Upward = 13 (25%)   Downward = 5 (10%)

Table IV–18

EDUCATIONAL MOBILITY FROM RESPONDENTS TO SONS OF RESPONDENTS IN RATU

Education of Respondents	Education of Sons (in Years)				
	10+	6–9	1–5	None	Total
10th Grade and above	—	—	—	—	—
6th to 9th Grade	—	2	—	—	2
1st to 5th Grade	2	—	—	1	3
None	1	1	2	13	17
Total	3	3	2	14	22

Mobile = 7 (32%)   Upward = 6 (27%)   Downward = 1 (5%)

Table IV–19

EDUCATIONAL MOBILITY FROM RESPONDENTS TO SONS OF RESPONDENTS IN BHAGU

Education of Respondents	Education of Sons (in Years)				
	10+	6–9	1–5	None	Total
10th Grade and above	—	—	—	—	—
6th to 9th Grade	—	—	—	—	—
1st to 5th Grade	—	2	1	2	5
None	—	2	4	7	13
Total	—	4	5	9	18

Mobile = 10 (56%)   Upward = 8 (45%)   Downward = 2 (11%)

Table IV–20

OCCUPATIONAL MOBILITY FROM FATHERS OF RESPONDENTS TO RESPONDENTS IN JAITI

Occupation of Fathers of Respondents	Occupation of Respondents				
	4	3	2	1	Total
1. Agricultural laborer	—	2	2	8	12
2. Farmer	6	3	133	9	151
3. Skilled and related	2	19	5	1	27
4. Professional and related	2	—	6	—	8
Total	10	24	146	18	198

Mobile = 36 (18%)   Upward = 15 (7%)   Downward = 21 (11%)

There were certain social structural factors which seemed to be associated with increasing educational mobility. The most important among them was the increased value placed on education. An increasing number of people adopted the norm that a better quality of life could be realized by more education. More people of all backgrounds were acquiring education in recent years. Another important structural factor is that there were a larger number of jobs available in the nonagricultural sector. A third factor is that people had more knowledge of such opportunities, a result of the village economy's failure to provide adequate means of livelihood for all of its members. Most jobs outside the village available to the people required some education and skill. Education thus facilitated general participation in the nonvillage environment. The current indications are that an increasing number of people will use whatever means are at their disposal to strive for more education for their sons, if not for themselves.

According to Tables IV–11 and IV–12, the correlations between occupations of fathers and respondents were .37 in Jaiti and .29 in Ratu. In Bhagu, due to no variance in the fathers' occupations, we did not find any correlation between the occupations of the two generations.

Tables IV–20, IV–21, and IV–22 show that some occupational mobility occurred from the generation of fathers to the generation of respondents. Occupational mobility was 27 percent in Ratu, 18 percent in Jaiti, and only 4 percent in Bhagu. In Ratu and Jaiti, downward mobility exceeded upward mobility. In Bhagu, out of the three mobile families, two moved up and one down. We must recognize that most people in Bhagu were farmers and there was little possibility, according to our ranking, for them to move down. Most of the downward mobility elsewhere was from nonagricultural occupations to agricultural occupations. Furthermore, most of those who moved into nonagricultural occupations had a farm background. These gains and losses between agricultural and nonagricultural occupations have generally balanced each other out. It is important to note that occupational mobility has occurred in both directions from the various occupational locations. Tables IV–23, IV–24 and IV–25 represent occupational mobility from the respondents to their sons. When we compared these with Tables IV–20, IV–21 and IV–22, we found that in the third generation there was greater occupational mobility than in the second generation. In Jaiti and Bhagu, the mobility from the respondents to their sons was entirely upward, while in Ratu it was slightly downward. Bhagu was still far behind in occupational mobility compared to Ratu and Jaiti.

Respondents who were in nonagricultural occupations were more likely to have sons in similar occupations. However, greater movement occurred from the lower to the higher occupations. Comparisons of occupational mobility tables showed that the diagonal cells had become proportionately smaller in the occupational tables of respondents and their sons, compared to the sizes of diagonal cells in the occupational tables of fathers and the respondents. These were indicative of the trend of increasing occupational mobility across generations, reflecting mainly shifts from agricultural to nonagricultural occupations. A father's nonagricultural occupational status origin influenced the occupation of sons more than a father's agricultural occupational status origin. In other words, the sons of fathers in nonagricultural occupations were likely to avoid downward mobility, while the sons of fathers in the agricultural occupations could only move up. These trends indicated that nonagricultural occupations would gain more people and nonagricultural mobility would take place largely between adjacent occupations. Agricultural occupations would continue to lose if there were continuing demands for labor in other occupations.

Table IV–21

OCCUPATIONAL MOBILITY FROM FATHERS OF RESPONDENTS TO RESPONDENTS
IN RATU

Occupation of Fathers of Respondents	Occupation of Respondents				
	4	3	2	1	Total
1. Agricultural laborer	—	1	1	3	5
2. Farmer	4	1	38	3	46
3. Skilled and related	—	4	5	—	9
4. Professional and related	1	—	2	—	3
Total	5	6	46	6	63

Mobile = 17 (27%)   Upward = 7 (11%)   Downward = 10 (16%)

Table IV–22

OCCUPATIONAL MOBILITY FROM FATHERS OF RESPONDENTS TO RESPONDENTS
IN BHAGU

Occupation of Fathers of Respondents	Occupation of Respondents				
	4	3	2	1	Total
1. Agricultural laborer	—	—	—	—	—
2. Farmer	2	—	64	1	67
3. Skilled and related	—	—	—	—	—
4. Professional and related	—	—	—	—	—
Total	2	—	64	1	67

Mobile = 3 (4%)   Upward = 2 (3%)   Downward = 1 (1%)

Table IV–23

OCCUPATIONAL MOBILITY FROM RESPONDENTS TO SONS OF RESPONDENTS
IN JAITI

Occupation of Respondents	Occupation of Sons				
	4	3	2	1	Total
1. Agricultural laborer	—	—	1	—	1
2. Farmer	9	2	30	—	41
3. Skilled and related	—	5	—	—	5
4. Professional and related	3	—	—	—	3
Total	12	7	31	—	50

Mobile = 12 (24%)   Upward = 12 (24%)   Downward = 0

Table IV–24

OCCUPATIONAL MOBILITY FROM RESPONDENTS TO SONS OF RESPONDENTS IN RATU

Occupation of Respondents	Occupation of Sons				
	4	3	2	1	Total
1. Agricultural laborer	—	—	1	2	3
2. Farmer	5	—	9	2	16
3. Skilled and related	—	3	—	—	3
4. Professional and related	—	—	—	—	—
Total	5	3	10	4	22

Mobile = 8 (36%)   Upward = 6 (27%)   Downward = 2 (9%)

Table IV–25

OCCUPATIONAL MOBILITY FROM RESPONDENTS TO SONS OF RESPONDENTS
IN BHAGU

Occupation of Respondents	Occupation of Sons				
	4	3	2	1	Total
1. Agricultural laborer	—	—	—	—	—
2. Farmer	1	—	16	—	17
3. Skilled and related	—	—	—	—	—
4. Professional and related	—	—	—	—	—
Total	1	—	16	—	17

Mobile = 1 (6%)   Upward = 1 (6%)   Downward = 0

Some social structural factors are suggested to explain the trends in occupational mobility. The amount of occupational mobility over generations followed the rank ordering of concentration of land in the villages. Ratu had the greatest concentration of land in the villages, and the greatest occupational mobility, while Bhagu showed the least concentration in landownership as well as the smallest amount of occupational mobility. The more differentiated the occupational structure of the village, the higher would be its potential occupational mobility. The number of educated persons increased over time. This made possible greater participation in nonagricultural occupations.

It was noted that the respondents from Ratu and Jaiti did not differ significantly in education, but the occupational mobility from fathers to respondents varied between the two villages. Part of this explanation was found in the differences within the caste structure of the villages. Jaiti is a high-caste village, and some high-caste people did not need to use their education to participate in nonagricultural occupations. In Ratu, there were larger numbers of people in the middle-range castes who moved out of their traditional occupations, and some of these joined nonagricultural occupations.

Both the lowest and the highest castes showed greater occupational stability between the fathers and the respondents. The middle-range castes were the most occupationally mobile. This pattern was found to be consistent over the three generations in these villages. Villages with a larger proportion of middle-range castes experienced greater intergenerational occupational mobility than villages with higher or lower castes. This trend changed somewhat in the third generation. Occupational mobility from respondents to their sons was generally in an upward direction, with sons finding employment in occupations higher than their fathers' to an increase in occupational opportunities for those with some education. The higher correlations between education and occupation in this generation suggested that this indeed was the explanation.

The evidence suggested then, that a family's caste, its extent of landholding, its occupational position, and its level of education provided some explanations for its occupational mobility. Such outside factors as availability of jobs in urban and industrial areas also influenced occupational mobility. The inability of the village economy to absorb the available labor force forced some people to find jobs outside the village. A few started petty trade in the village itself. In the third generation, higher castes joined the middle-range castes in participating in nonagricultural occupations. The size of landholding of the family had become less important in the occupational choices of the sons of the respondents. The influence of education on occupational choice increased in the sons' generation.

In the most recent generation, educational and occupational mobility increased more than in the past. It appeared as though a father's caste and landholdings were less important factors in motivating his son's educational and occupational achievements than were the father's own educational and occupational achievements. As more villagers moved into nonagricultural occupations, the correlations between education and occupation also increased. The increasing importance of an individual's father's education and occupation on his educational and occupational choices did not automatically mean that caste would have lower associations with educational and occupational choices. We simply argue that participation in higher education and occupations became less determined by one's caste status or landholdings. A family's caste and land became potential resources, along with educational and occupational statuses, to influence the educational and occupational mobility of subsequent generations.

THE TWO-CLASS SYSTEM

The zamindari system made the top positions in each community accessible largely through status ascription during 1930–46. The intercorrelations for the respondents' generation were very much like those of their fathers, and it was not until the generation of the sons of respondents that a new stratification system began to take shape. In the latter, both ascriptive and achievement variables were highly correlated wherever caste structure was differentiated.

During the respondents' generation, zamindari was abolished, contact between rural and urban economic sectors was intensified, education increased, and the villagers became able to understand important aspects of new legal provisions and other institutional changes. These changes added new ground rules for the status attainment process. The reality of everyday life and the impact of some of these changes were reflected only minimally in intergenerational correlations.

One would expect that the association between stratification variables in previous generations would be high and that the forces of change would diminish the intercorrelations in each subsequent generation. We found almost a reverse trend. The emerging stratification system was certainly more ordered and probably more rigid than the previous ones. In the emerging system such achievement-based variables as level of education and occupational status were more closely associated with such ascriptive variables as caste status and property status than was the case two generations earlier.

The nature and the magnitude of intercorrelations between stratification variables during the fathers' generation showed the simplicity of the system. The key to the stratification system during 1930–46 lay in the tremendous economic and political power of the higher-caste zamindars. They were members of judicial tribunals. They acted as intermediaries between the village people and the outside world. In addition to traditions and conventions, their power was reinforced by support from the police, revenue officials and other administrators. We have designated these men at the apex of the stratification system as the "community influentials." The position of this group was largely hereditary; very little change had occurred in its composition.

In Jaiti, a rare example of achieved status attainment occurred. A Brahmin bought property from some minor zamindars some years ago and used it as a qualification to enter the ranks of the community influentials. His family was accorded less prestige and esteem from the people in comparison to those who were the descendants of rich zamindars for several generations. However, the numerical strength and aggressiveness of the Brahmin's kin, his knowledge of laws and his higher-caste status helped him to enter the group of community influentials to exercise power. The advent of the newly powerful Brahmin led to the formation of factions among the influentials and created an atmosphere of suspicion and divisiveness. Despite the consequent lack of internal cohesion, however, this group continued to enjoy the highest power and prestige during 1930–46.

In Ratu, initially a Brahmin and a Kshatriya family constituted the class of community influentials. They were zamindars with a considerable amount of land who had some education and did not do any agricultural work themselves. The Kshatriya family owned the entire village several generations ago but the mismanagement of land and lack of knowledge of property laws forced it to give up large amounts of land. By the middle of the 1930's much of the land had been sold to an ᵃʰsentee Muslim zamindar and some to two Brahmin zamindars of Jaiti and one local Brahmin zamindar, but the family still owned enough land to maintain its power and prestige. The spokesman of a locally dominant caste which claimed its ritual status closer to that of the Brahmins than other castes was accepted as a minor member of the community influentials on the understanding that he would help to implement the decisions of the somewhat weakened group. As in the former example, the addition of a new member was definitely considered to be an exception to policy.

Bhagu, being a predominantly lower-caste village, had a more heterogeneous group of community influentials than the other two villages. A Kshatriya family which held the position of traditional village-head and two lower-caste families comprised the class of community influentials, although one representative of an absentee landlord was consulted in important matters. The three families belonged to upper landholding groups and were not too compulsive about the indignity of hard physical labor. One of the lower-caste influentials was illiterate. This group was less autonomous than its counterparts in the other villages and consulted the zamindars of Jaiti on important matters. The support of higher-caste influentials from the neighboring village also assured that police, revenue and other officials would not interfere in local matters. This suggested that higher ritual status gave confidence to the local influentials and enabled them to act more effectively.

In every case a few persons who were predominantly higher-caste, or were spokesmen of dominant castes, who possessed relatively larger amounts of land, who had some education, and who avoided physical labor, constituted the class of community influentials. They did not always act in unison but they resisted any attempts by the outsiders to enter their ranks. Despite bitter internal competition for power and prestige, they all acted in favor of upholding the caste norms. They ignored the moral issue of intimidation and exploitation of lower castes by higher castes. They used persuasion and, if that failed, coercion to deal with any opposition. All were members of judicial tribunals which guaranteed them great power and the support of the government officials. The hereditary principle of recruitment helped maintain intergenerational stability in the composition of this group.

The remaining members of each community were more hetereo-geneous on all dimensions of stratification than the community intel-lectuals, but they had one thing in common: the inability to affect the outcome of important community matters. Members of higher castes had superior status (as did landholders) than those who lacked land or high-caste status, but they did not act in local matters independently of community influentials. They were used by the latter to carry out their wishes with minimum opposition. Sometimes, court litigations were manufactured in which some community in-fluentials gave moral and/or material support to embarrass other in-fluentials. Despite these antagonistic internal attitudes, the influen-tials rarely allowed any of their outside supporters to join their ranks.

The major function of community influentials was to maintain peace and order. If anyone questioned their authority, they resorted to economic boycott, physical assaults, and intimidation through the police or other government officials. There was considerable predic-tability in the system and people went about their business with little community concern because all matters were handled by the com-munity influentials. In the village projects, persons from the lower castes contributed labor and higher castes supervised and gave food to the laborers, while the community influentials made decisions about who did what. Family and caste disputes were settled by influentials on the basis of local norms. Property disputes and assault cases were decided by the influentials in cooperation with revenue and police officials, although serious matters might be taken to the courts. Out-siders could not elicit information or receive help from the local cit-izenry until they were duly identified by one of the community influentials.

The postindependence changes were intended to alter traditional relations, enhance greater participation of people in the economic and political systems, and lessen inequality. The results were mixed. Ritual, economic and power inequality declined, and educational and occupational inequality increased, although more and more peo-ple from the depressed groups took advantage of educational and occupational opportunities.

The higher association among the stratification variables in the third generation, of sons of respondents, indicated that despite equali-tarian principles, the pattern of inequality had become more ordered. Those who were in advantageous positions in the community used their resources to acquire higher status on achievement-based dimen-sions. The lower comparability of positions on various dimensions of status in the previous generations was mainly due to lack of educa-tion and availability of nonagricultural occupations. In the third generation, educational and occupational opportunities expanded, but some were better equipped to take advantage of them than others, pointing to the fact that equalitarian principles did not by themselves guarantee improvement in the status of depressed groups. Those at the apex of the stratification system successfully managed to maintain their positions. Others with material resources and motivation tried to better themselves.

Unlike the previous stratification system, the emerging system does not rest solely on ascription, but ascriptive positions are skillfully used to acquire higher educational and occupational status. Higher-caste persons realize that the only way to maintain their higher prestige is to do better under the new system. The ability to stay at the top is made possible by their superior property status and the income it affords for acquiring education and consequently entering higher occupations. The community influentials are no longer an exclusive group. Membership in the class of community influentials does not rest entirely on ascription, and some new persons have begun to claim membership in it.

The reputational method was used to study the class structure in the postindependence period. We interviewed random samples of 22 percent of our respondents in Jaiti, 27 percent in Ratu and 24 percent in Bhagu. Each caste in each village was represented. We asked the respondents to identify the "most important and influential persons" in their villages. Once they identified these men, we asked them to name those who were active in giving advice or acting as mediators in such matters as family or caste disputes and legal matters and in contacting lawyers or government departments on behalf of residents in negotiations involving police, revenue or agricultural development matters. Each identified person in these areas received a score on each issue on the basis of the number of respondents who mentioned his name. A high score indicated that in addition to having earned prestige and esteem from his fellow villagers, he also made important decisions affecting the village. Therefore, this group was labelled as community influentials during the postindependence period.

Tables IV–26, IV–27 and IV–28 showed that in each village persons identified as "important and influential" differed in caste status, property status and level of education. There were 24 such persons in Jaiti, 10 in Ratu and 14 in Bhagu. Of these, 15 persons in Jaiti and six each in Ratu and Bhagu monopolized the advisory as well as decision-making roles in important matters, The rest were identified as important and influential for reasons other than their being active influentials in the village. The relative power and prestige of each family in the village was known to the villagers. Some additional names appeared because each caste named its spokesman and some even added their personal friends irrespective of their power and prestige.

Table IV-26

INTERCORRELATIONS OF PARTICIPATION AMONG ISSUE-AREAS FOR THE COMMUNITY INFLUENTIALS DURING 1947–65 IN JAITI

	1	2	3	4	5	6	7	8	9	10	11	12
1. Caste		.14	.55	.38	.29	.18	.34	.33	.27	.28	.32	.16
2. Land		—	.45	.55	.50	.36	.72	.78	.65	.19	.72	.17
3. Education				.57	.62	.55	.42	.43	.34	.50	.22	.61
4. Mentioned Influential					.82	.68	.85	.83	.84	.64	.67	.63
5. Family Dispute						.95	.87	.85	.89	.90	.58	.91
6. Caste Dispute							.71	.73	.80	.91	.31	.97
7. Legal Matters								.95	.95	.66	.88	.61
8. Contacting Lawyers									.96	.57	.82	.58
9. Contacting Govt.										.72	.77	.67
10. Police Matters											.30	.96
11. Revenue Matters												.22
12. Development Matters												—

Table IV-27

INTERCORRELATIONS OF PARTICIPATION AMONG ISSUE-AREAS FOR THE COMMUNITY INFLUENTIALS DURING 1947–65 IN RATU

	1	2	3	4	5	6	7	8	9	10	11	12
1. Caste		.67	.63	.87	.46	.27	.18	.03	.27	.15	.18	.75
2. Land		—	.62	.39	.46	.21	-.35	-.21	-.09	-.25	-.20	-.94
3. Education				.42	.42	.18	-.10	.04	.54	-.16	-.21	-.61
4. Mentioned Influential					.44	.55	.63	.76	.82	.70	.78	-.10
5. Family Dispute						.67	.54	.53	-.08	-.35	.08	-.19
6. Caste Dispute							.89	.82	.63	.49	.07	-.23
7. Legal Matters								.98	.70	.51	.73	.37
8. Contacting Lawyers									.76	.56	.79	.20
9. Contacting Govt.										.96	.94	.02
10. Police Matters											.88	-.09
11. Revenue Matters												-.20
12. Development Matters												—

Table IV-28

INTERCORRELATIONS OF PARTICIPATION AMONG ISSUE-AREAS FOR THE COMMUNITY INFLUENTIALS DURING 1947–65 IN BHAGU

	1	2	3	4	5	6	7	8	9	10	11	12
1. Caste	—	.14	-.20	.25	.04	-.23	-.10	.04	-.30	-.20	-.10	-.25
2. Land			.23	.11	-.54	-.38	-.62	-.52	-.78	-.77	-.69	-.79
3. Education				.20	-.35	-.30	-.41	-.46	-.40	-.41	-.48	-.41
4. Mentioned Influential					.69	.64	.67	.70	.57	.67	.68	.62
5. Family Dispute						.96	.99	.98	.98	.99	.99	.98
6. Caste Dispute							.99	.96	.99	.99	.98	.99
7. Legal Matters								.99	.99	.99	.99	.99
8. Contacting Lawyers									.97	.97	.99	.96
9. Contacting Govt.										.99	.99	.99
10. Police Matters											.99	1.00
11. Revenue Matters												1.00
12. Development Matters												.99
												—

Higher associations between various scores for the names submitted as important and influential persons were found in Jaiti and Bhagu than occurred in Ratu: the former were domiated by higher and lower castes respectively. The life-styles in Jaiti and Bhagu were well-defined and local norms had high degrees of acceptance and stability; this resulted in the nomination of a well-defined group of men who wielded power and were accorded prestige in each village.

In Jaiti, coercion and manipulation were used to maintain power and prestige, and those who exercised them were easily recognized. In Bhagu, however, an emphasis on consensus and cooperation as the most valued characteristics of leadership facilitated recognition of the influentials. In Ratu, on the other hand, a mixed-caste culture existed in which middle-range castes shared power with higher castes, and lower castes had begun to challenge some of the middle-range caste leaders. This generated a more diffuse group of influentials because some were active only in certain kinds of situations. Mutual suspicion was widespread in Ratu, and there was not a single well integrated group that commanded superior status to all persons at all times. These differences influenced the class structure of the three villages. Ratu had a less well defined class of community influentials than Jaiti or Bhagu. Despite some differences, the people of Ratu still acknowledged the existence of a broad class of persons containing all those who were accorded greater power and prestige. Everyone acknowledged the existence of a "power elite," each of whom on some occasions determined the outcomes of important events.

The class of community influentials in each of the villages was different in certain respects from its counterpart in the preindependence period. It was no longer exclusively composed of higher-caste persons with higher property status and greater access to the good things of life. Those who had the support of a numerically dominant group and had political skills managed to infiltrate the ranks of community influentials. Those families that had been influential in the past continued to maintain their position, showing a marked stability across time. The addition of new influentials did not affect the superior status of the old families, but they became more tactful and cautious in exercising their power. Occasionally, concrete legal action on the part of the landless and the lower castes forced the old community influentials to come to grips with new realities. Such an action resulted in the redistribution of land in Jaiti and Ratu, while the consensus-oriented community influentials of Bhagu did not encounter similar direct confrontations.

The evidence clearly indicated that in the class system of post-independence, the principle of achievement had begun to influence the process of recruitment to the class of influentials. The relatively closed class system of the preindependence period was different from the new class system, even though the community influentials of the past succeeded in maintaining their superior position. The emerging stratification showed marked continuity with the previous stratification system, but the new class of influentials was drawn from a broader spectrum of the village community. Both ascription and achievement influenced the stratification system in complex ways, although a growing trend towards the latter was observed.

STATUS CONSISTENCY

The imperfect associations among the stratification dimensions suggests the existence of status inconsistency. It should be stated that status inconsistency was tolerated and, in some contexts, even admired in traditional India. For instance, only three decades ago, a Brahmin who worshipped and spent most of his time in reading and writing but did not have large landholdings, commanded respect from the people. Similarly, an individual of lower-caste status or someone from the middle-range castes could quite legitimately raise his economic status by working hard — as long as he did not attempt to change the traditional order. Many people, including some from higher castes, had inconsistent statuses. Access to property, educational, and occupational statuses varied widely within each caste even though each member enjoyed equal ritual status. Lower-caste people were usually low on all dimensions of status, but a few families improved their property status, level of education, and occupational status by such legitimate devices as working for the railways — an activity not associated with any traditional castes. Most examples of status inconsistency were to be found among individuals of the upper castes rather than among the middle or lower castes.

The stability of the caste system over time tended to minimize status inconsistency. The caste system supported traditional social and economic relations. During the fathers' generation we noted that as long as a few higher-caste people monopolized ecoonmic power, had some education, and did not do manual jobs, the majority of higher-caste people believed in the system, even when they derived no advantage other than higher ritual status from it. The high-caste poor, for instance, claimed superior status merely by emphasizing their ritual ranks. Such claims were supported by local traditions, and were recognized by government officials and higher-caste visitors to their villages.

Lower-caste persons who had improved their economic conditions refrained deliberately from displaying their material gains in their own villages. Even so, they earned the esteem of their caste and kinship groups. A higher-caste illiterate man did not go to a lower-caste literate man to seek help in reading and writing — for him to do so would have embarrassed the latter. A lower-caste illiterate man would be constrained to seek help from a higher-caste person rather than from someone of his own ritual rank. In such ways the traditional order was validated. Deviations might have been sanctioned by a social and economic boycott of the offender.

Some lower-caste men who had achieved success in nonascriptive areas during the preindependence period sought community-wide recognition through the approval of higher-caste influential men. The greater their humility regarding their secular achievements, the greater was the approval from all sections of the community. The access to higher economic, educational and occupational statuses was legitimate for the middle-range castes, yet they were more status-consistent than any other group in these communities.

Bhagu, being a largely lower-caste village, showed some interesting features. The numerical dominance of lower castes resulted in the breakdown of certain caste norms. These deviations caused some degree of uproar outside of the village, but for the people within the community it did not matter much. The higher-caste deviants were not ridiculed or abandoned by their caste fellows, because the community was dominated by a lower-caste culture in which such acts were tolerated. In an intercommunity context, the higher-caste people of Bhagu avoided interaction with higher-caste people of other communities; the latter often talked with contempt about the former. Prior to independence, status inconsistency was inconsequential as long as caste members maintained their relative positions in the traditional order. The stability and acceptance of ritual ranking enabled people to cope with inconsistent statuses without any serious dislocations.

Lower-caste persons who acquired education, obtained better occupations and became economically independent usually avoided interaction with higher-caste people. The latter generally did not recognize the newly acquired statuses. Lower-caste people had begun to shift their world views from the traditional local scene to the national panorama, with its major centers of economic and political power. They had already started to readjust their way of life according to the demands of new political and economic institutions. Enthusiasm for social change began to grow within the lower castes. Most higher-caste people were either indifferent to or opposed to drastic institutional changes. The middle-range castes were ambivalent; they were in favor of contemporary changes but they felt that the lower castes were "getting out of hand" and that there might be serious conflicts in the future.

As the definition of India's new social order struggled to come into being, many high-caste persons tried to improve their educational and economic statuses so that these would become consistent with the emergent higher social ranks. Higher-caste people, for instance, invested more in education and used their contacts outside the community to get better jobs for their children. Previously, most higher-caste people were generally content as long as some of their caste fellows monopolized economic power and maintained the traditional order; but now the situation had changed, and most of them were trying to compete for high status independently.

Prior to independence, caste status was relevant in social relations, and status inconsistency did not cause any serious social structural or psychological problems. But after independence, coping with status inconsistency became more problematic because official pronouncements and actions weakened the importance of caste status in interpersonal relations. The avoidance behavior or occasional acts of confrontation and violence within the communities seemed temporary. People of higher-caste background began to acquire more education and higher occupational status to reduce status inconsistency, while lower-caste people concentrated on their efforts to acquire land and education, and to participate in nonagricultural occupations. Young men who were not satisfied with their lower ritual status thought of moving out of the village. The middle-range castes were least troubled because they generally experienced less status inconsistency from the past to the present. Caste status continued to be an important aspect of the stratification system, but greater acceptance of other kinds of status made the status system more open. However, despite the fact that it is responding to increased urbanization and industrialization in a predicted fashion, the stratification system of India will still maintain certain social structural pecularities, at least for some time.

The findings of this research describe some features of the life and life chances of those Indians who are the victims of centuries-old social disabilities. With greater social, economic, and political freedom with independence, and some material and moral support from the government, it is expected that these people will eventually succeed in upgrading themselves. But at present this has not occurred. In this period higher-caste people were more likely to be found in higher educational and occupational strata than lower-caste people. The emerging system of inequality based on achievement is in accord with the caste inequality. In Bhagu where higher-caste influence was minimal, and lower-caste groups exercised greater freedom, people did not make much progress in their educational and occupational achievement when compared with the higher-caste people in Ratu and Jaiti.

NOTES

1. Generally when a correlation was higher than .39 it was considered "higher", when it ranged between .20 and .39 it was designated "medium", and "lower" was below .20.

Part Five

Some Conclusions and Theoretical Applications

Support for the disappearance of caste stratification in India may be found by studying certain populations. Support for the persistence of the caste system may be found by studying others. A more homogeneous community (in terms of caste) exhibits fewer ritual distinctions than one which has a more differentiated caste structure. In addition to caste, there are other important dimensions of stratification in India. From a broad perspective, some important implications of recent changes that have occurred to rural stratification in India have been reviewed. In the previous chapters the prevailing tendency to shift from a more ascriptive and closed stratification system to a more achievement-based and open stratification system has been noted. The implication has been that an individual's position is determined less and less by caste status and inherited property and more and more by his own ability to accumulate property or other forms of wealth, his level of education and occupational status. He may improve his economic status by working in urban and industrial occupations and then buying land with his earnings. He may also choose to invest in the education of his children in the hope of improving family status in the long run. Disadvantaged persons may improve their status by acquiring more wealth and by increasing motivation for competition and success. These devices tend to break the interdependence of ascriptive and achievement-based sources of higher status in the emerging stratification system.

It will take some time for the depressed groups to experience drastic changes in status, and they are not in a mood to accept the traditional order. Their success depends upon the actions and achievements of those who were at the top in the past and who are also determined to maintain their position in the emerging stratification system. The indications are that the nature of the emerging stratification will be qualitatively distinct, although certain of its elements may still continue to persist.

Neither the functionalist nor the conflict theories of stratification can fully explain the changes in the stratification system of these communities. The domination of the zamindar group on the basis of ownership of property, and the importance of caste status during the pre-independence period, have been undermined with the legal abolition of the zamindari system, and the establishment of local panchayats after independence. The emerging stratification system cannot be properly understood if one insists upon fitting the facts to one particular theory.

The discussions in Part IV indicated that both conflict and functionalist notions are useful in understanding changes in the stratification system. For instance, prior to independence, the zamindar-tenant relationship rested on the ownership of property, but at the same time the caste system played an important part in determining the general profile of the stratification system. After independence, the government intervened and deliberately tried to change the principles of inequality in such a way that ascription played as little a role as possible and certain disadvantaged groups received preferential treatment. The aim was to integrate various segments of the population into the new ideals of democratic socialism.

The above examples suggest that a multidimensional approach would be more appropriate for studying stratification and that the main purpose of such studies should not be to test a theory but to describe the data. If these data lean towards a particular theory, only then can it be said that it explains the stratification system in a given historical and social structural context. This caution is even more necessary for those societies in which the stratification system has yet to be systematically studied.

As discussed earlier, a conflict theory better describes the stratification system prior to independence. The zamindars controlled the means of production and exploited other groups for their own self-interest. Other elements in the status system, however, cannot be explained by conflict theory.

In the postindependence period, the influential families of the past continued to be important but their ranks expanded. Expertise, skill and efficiency now greatly influence access to power and prestige in keeping with functional theory. Community influentials are under constant pressure to promote equality and maintain peace and order in an atmosphere of scarcity and mistrust. Under these conditions, the stratification system will be more open in the future, and enterprising individuals will have opportunities to compete for power and prestige.

The role of caste inequality in the general stratification system depends upon the local social, economic, and political structures. The indications are that its influence will become more and more indirect and secondary. In the next few pages we will describe the general implications of the findings of this study and some other issues as well.

Recent changes in the economic and political systems of India have affected traditional social relations. The once weak and docile lower castes have begun to unite and fight for their economic and political rights. If they succeed, their next target may be to attack the caste system as a measurement of social status. They will insist that instead of caste, such factors as income, education and occupation should be used for determining social standing. The response of higher-caste people towards attempts to weaken the caste system may be neither agreeable nor uniform. Some of them may adopt a philosophical view that whatever is happening cannot be stopped, while others may claim a superior status, avoiding open confrontations with the "nonbelievers". Many who have the resources and motivation would rather devote their energies to competing for higher education and occupations than to indulging in fruitless quarrels, realizing that the trend to weaken the caste system cannot be reversed under the current political climate. In contrast, there are those higher-caste persons who avoid competition where they are not confident of their superiority and those who resort to intimidation and violence to "keep the lower castes in their places."

The numerically dominant castes will exploit their strength either through occupying local political offices or by acting as important pressure groups. The village panchayats and cooperative societies are constituted of elected representatives. They are responsible for local planning and development. They make decisions regarding the utilization of local resources, as well as grants and subsidies advanced by the government. Two important consequences of participation in government by the lower castes, especially in leadership positions, are that they will be better treated by others socially, and that they will have opportunities to pass judgment on the conduct of upper-caste people. Therefore, numerical dominance has become an important means of diminishing ascriptive social and political inequality. It also enables the lower castes to demand their full share in economic resources. Even those who are not numerically dominant act as pressure groups, and enter into political alliances with others to protect their interests.

Continued progress in social and political equality will depend upon the rate of economic betterment of lower castes and other poor segments of the population. Help from the government will not be enough to improve the living conditions of all depressed groups or to eliminate the economic disparities between them and others.

It is sometimes suggested that once the lower castes become economically well-off, they will claim superior caste status in the local caste hierarchy. They will enhance their ritual status through the process of Sanskritization. This line of reasoning implies that there are pressures for status congruency. However, greater inequality in general status may continue to exist despite increased mobility. Through Sanskritization, an individual is unable to separate himself from his castefellows, in an attempt to improve his personal status. Even if we accept that the process of Sanskritization will be attractive to depressed groups, we do not find it a practical means for achieving higher status. Most lower castes collectively lack economic resources, the most important requirement for successful Sanskritization.

Westernization has been considered as another alternative for the lower castes and other poor; it would mainly involve acquisition of Western education, participation in nontraditional occupations, and adaption to such norms as competition and individual autonomy. There is a possibility for the lower castes to improve their general status outside the realm of the traditional caste system through this process. We expect that the removal of legal disabilities and the greater opportunities for educational and occupational participation will motivate lower-caste people to choose Westernization as the route to improve their general status without considering Sanskritization as a necessary step. This process will be primarily individual rather than collective. Perhaps Westernizing lower castes will act as a group to bring changes into the system when they find that they as individuals face organized opposition from other groups. The rural economic structure and their social and economic status within the community will force the lower castes to search for economic opportunities outside the rural sector. Social and political equality will prove ineffective in improving the standard of living of these people when economic resources are scarce in the community. There is not much to be distributed.

The lower castes are not fighting for equality without support. They have their sympathizers in the regional, state and national political parties as well as in the village communities. The secret of their support lies in an ability to work as unified political groups in elections. The system of universal adult suffrage has provided the most powerful weapon of all: their votes. The caste leaders in the past helped perpetrate the caste system by punishing the violators of intercaste taboos. Now, the same leaders realize that their inherited ritual status should not have been the basis for social and economic exploitation. The defiant mood of the lower castes will grow stronger, demonstrated by block-voting for those candidates who are sympathetic to their cause.

Attacks on the legitimacy of a traditional system undermine the roots of hitherto unquestioned exploitation. For example, one source of moral degradation has been the practice of labeling some occupations as defiling: barber, washerman, tanner, and handler of dead animals. Many people have begun to abandon these occupations after finding other alternatives for making a living. Those who perform them demand more rewards, and may even insist that the defiling connotation of their services be dropped, while also asking that the relationship between themselves and their clients be considered contractual.

The traditional belief that inferiority and exploitation of lower-caste people is morally right is being questioned; thus, a serious upheaval of the traditional social, economic and political scenes is in the making. The traditional loyalty to ex-masters or clients will progressively disappear, especially as a result of organized actions by those of both secular and nonsecular affinities. No longer will the performance of manual and other specialized low occupations be reserved for certain castes. In fact, those who perform demeaning jobs insist that their employers should work with them to counteract the centuries-old stigma attached to these occupations. Employers, who in the past exploited cheap labor, have begun to face the problems of higher wages and the demands for respectful treatment in the work situation. As most employers have only small landholdings it may be difficult for many of them to bear the cost of increased wages. In the absence of suitable alternatives, employers will have to work on their own land and — most degrading of all — drag their own dead cattle.

The higher castes will continue to constitute the larger proportions of the higher economic stratum. Although caste will indirectly influence the composition of strata and classes, the economic rationale will push people to seek greater economic advantages that will eventually lead to greater heterogeneity in each stratum or class, but there is no guarantee that those with higher caste and economic backgrounds will maintain their superiority. The ranks of community influentials will become more open and competitive. What will happen to the mass of people below this class is anybody's guess. Indications are that the new wave of competitive spirit will divide them into several distinct classes with greater mobility, both upward and downward. The new economic system favors those who have acquired an education, and who are cognizant of the use of political favors for preferential treatment in job recruitment.

Many smaller landholders may move to urban areas in order to find steady employment. The pressure of growing families and the scarcity of land will force many people to look for alternative economic opportunities in both rural and urban areas. The opportunity for higher-caste people to live in relatively anonymous urban environments and work at lower occupations for economic survival will alleviate embarrassment. The lower castes have less to lose by moving to the city, and these new urban dwellers may develop broader communities among themselves to meet some of their social needs. Needless to say, not all who want to will get the opportunity to move to urban areas, or to live in the village while working in the city. Those who are forced to remain in the village will have to expand their landholdings, or work for someone else as a laborer or a share-cropper to meet their economic needs.

It should be pointed out that if the Indian economy fails to grow rapidly, there will not be sufficient new jobs to absorb the surplus labor force. The rate of unemployment in both the rural and urban sectors will continue to rise, leaving many people without any option other than to make the best out of wherever they are located in the economic system. This situation, plus a basic unwillingness to relinquish property, will make land more valuable than ever before. The consequences of such conditions will be twofold: one, general poverty will continue to prevail, and secondly, disadvantaged groups will be doomed once more to their misfortunes and will have to give up their hopes of improvement. But even this will not necessarily cause a reversion to a rigid caste system or mean that caste will become an all-pervasive phenomenon in the stratification system. Rather, it is expected that economic status will become more important in determining general status and the wealthy will exploit the poor, irrespective of their caste status. In other words, those who exploit and those who are exploited will form more heterogeneous groups than they did in the past, although the former will still tend to exploit lower-caste people.

One of the most important developments during the past two decades has been the increased interaction between rural and urban populations due to greater communication facilities and the opportunity to participate in economic and political activities. The increased role of governmental (and a few nongovernmental) agencies has exposed the rural areas to effective urban influences. The regular visits or presence of doctors, engineers, technicians, nurses, and various other government personnel will help to develop a more diversified occupational structure in the rural communities. The expansion in education will also affect rural areas. It is expected that a set of new or modified social norms will be introduced by the educated young men. As a result of all these outside influences and stimulants, the village people may assign greater importance to higher educational and occupational achievement. Prestige will increasingly be assigned on the basis of differential education, skill, and income.

Despite the growing communication between rural and urban areas, some rural occupational groups can enter the urban centers with greater ease than others. Demands for such services as those of carpenters, blacksmiths, barbers, washermen and shoemakers have increased everywhere, and those who have the skills are able to take advantage of these opportunities. For example, herdsmen have joined milk co-operatives in order to sell their milk at a higher price and to ensure that it has a stable market. There are others who have begun to grow cash crops and sell them in the nearest market or the city. The traditional trading families have enlarged their businesses and have good future business prospects. Most of the above groups fall within the middle range of the caste hierarchy, those who belong neither to the lower castes nor to the higher-caste subcultures. Historically, their caste position in the broader community has never quite been defined, due to their contacts with people of various caste ranks.

Both higher and lower castes, on the other hand, have fewer job alternatives outside the village. The less educated in these groups generally lack the special skills that are saleable to urban environments. The relatively wealthy and educated higher-caste people prefer white-collar occupations in the urban areas, while still maintaining a liaison with the village where their former statuses are more strongly supported. The higher-caste poor appear more willing to work in lower-level occupations than in the past, but show a preference for impersonal and anonymous environments, such as large factories, shops or government bureaucracies. The people belonging to the lower castes who lack special skills tend to work in manual occupations and stop-gap arrangements. However, some of them have benefited by the preferential treatment they have received from the government. Lower-caste persons willing to take up any job are more adaptable to total urban environments than the higher castes, as to them the city is less hostile and discriminating than the village.

Higher-caste people, trying to take advantage of both the rural and the urban environments, have begun investing more and more in the education of their children, with the hope that once again they will occupy the upper echelons of the occupational structure. There is no doubt that persons possessing education and technical skills will have more economic opportunities in both rural and urban areas.

Currently, in rural areas, economic development is producing a demand for various kinds of specialists to repair agricultural implements, bicycles, radios, watches, etc. Architects, skilled carpenters, blacksmiths and bricklayers will also be increasingly needed. As a result, tailors, shopkeepers and traders will thrive in their business enterprises. As indicated before, most of these skills will come from the middle-range castes who have had a less well defined status, both in caste and traditional economic structures. In the rural areas, the lower castes will face greater difficulties. The continuing increase in the labor force, the decrease in the number of manual jobs, and their general lack of special skills will make life even more difficult.

Undoubtedly, a large percentage of the current, urban labor force which has a rural background will continue to maintain contacts with the rural areas. However, future generations may feel less strongly about having a rural economic or social base, and they will in all probability develop organizations for their betterment. Their identification with their caste may not totally disappear, but may, rather, develop into broad-based caste groups. Regional and linguistic divisions, however, will continue to persist within each caste community. These communities will tend to be more tolerant regarding the rules of purity and pollution, and allow intercaste social relations, including intermarriage. It should be added that these organized caste communities, even in the urban environment, will be found mainly among the lower-caste people, who fear being excluded on a social basis by people of higher ranks. The higher castes will have no need to organize themselves, as they will have access to the people of their own communities in the urban areas, as well as active contacts with their village relatives.

Caste groups will not only serve a social purpose, but will also enhance and provide greater economic and political participation for their members. Lower castes have a great deal to gain by resorting to organized group tactics. It should be noted that these lower-caste groups will show "interest group" characteristics rather than emphasizing the ritual aspects of the caste system. In fact, they may even reject the idea of their lower status by ascription and concentrate solely on achieving economic and political betterment. This emphasis on achievement does not exclude the possibility of their cooperation with various groups and individuals such as the neighborhood social clubs and singing and theatrical groups. They may, however, at the same time, work together with other groups in labor unions, cooperatives, political parties and the like. In other words, secular participation is more likely to increase with a caste via activity between various groups and individuals. This trend will set the stage for less correspondence between caste status and other stratification dimensions, although they will continue to be related to some extent.

There are two factors which may weaken the sense of caste identity: first, the development of and identification with the occupational community; and second, relatively uninhibited intercaste relations, resulting in personal friendship based on equality and eventually in a loosening of commensal rules and even in intermarriage. Neither of these factors seem likely to exert a significant influence in the next decade or two. However, emergence of an occupational community and weakening of the caste community will influence each other in complex ways, leading to increased participation in many areas of life, primarily those based upon secular principles.

When people of heterogeneous caste backgrounds work together it will be difficult to observe traditional caste rules. In the absence of economic and political sanctions, it will be more and more difficult to define caste status; in fact, caste names may become totally unfamiliar to many people. The lower castes are expected to reject those traditions and conventions that will put them in a position to be exploited by other caste groups. As indicated before, even though they may identify and organize themselves on caste lines for greater economic and political equality, their strategies should not be interpreted as an adherance to the caste system itself. They will, in fact, do everything possible to break the correspondence between caste status, economic status, political power and prestige.

The increasing interrelationship between education and occupation will motivate people in larger numbers to acquire more education. Although not all educated persons are able to find suitable jobs, they still have more occupational opportunities than the uneducated. Education will continue to expand without guaranteeing its equal accessibility to various groups or individuals. It is expected that the higher castes will continue to have more education than others. The expansion of education will narrow the gaps in educational inequality, generally at precollege levels, while the disparities may actually increase at higher educational levels. With the decline of traditional sources of higher status, higher castes will invest more and more in their children's educations. This is one undisputed factor that they can use to maintain their superiority in the changing Indian society.

The castes in the middle range of the hierarchy have a tradition of being literate; sometimes they have better literacy rates than higher castes. It seems that they will continue to emphasize their literacy, as it is important to conduct petty trade and business efficiently, but they may not indulge in the higher educational pursuits. On the other hand, in the absence of trade or business opportunities they can acquire higher education with considerable ease. They have the money, tradition and motivation for education. The lower castes, on the other hand, lack the economic resources as well as the motivation to take advantage of educational opportunities.

Although some lower-caste people will benefit from subsidized education and special programs, many will not be able even then to meet the costs of education, thus leaving the acquisition of education for the most part to those with higher economic status. It can be said that the lower castes will not make much headway in educational achievements unless adequate attempts are made to enable their children to go to school. In many poor families, the older children look after the younger ones. Often, they assist the family in agricultural operations as well. The indications are that lower-caste persons will have more literates but they will be concentrated in the lower educational brackets. Small grants for educational supplies, tuition waivers and the few scholarships available will not immediately make up for the disadvantages accrued from centuries of deprivation. Some revolutionary ideology may be necessary to make lower-caste participation in the educational system more realistic.

Many who work in the village or city are not fully employed. Migration of village labor means that, in addition to the educated, growing numbers of less qualified people are seeking employment in urban and industrial centers. Most rural migrants are from the middle and lower-caste groups — who have very little to lose by leaving the village. Middle and lower-caste groups care little about the prestige of occupations and prefer to work and live in an anonymous urban enviroment, as the wages are generally higher. There they can escape the occasional harrassment from their village employers who usually belong to higher castes. Despite their migration for equality and justice, the lack of economic opportunities still renders them vulnerable to economic disadvantages and exploitation.

Various government projects have been attracting more and more lower-caste people, despite a paucity of permanent jobs. However, the complexity of urban life and the insecurity of the job market force recollections, albeit with some cynicism, of the positive aspects of the zamindari system — particularly the help received from zamindars during critical times. The lower-caste dilemma is complex. In urban and industrial settings, their lack of education keeps them behind. In the villages, there are insufficient opportunities to improve their social and economic status. In addition, they do not have good contacts, which are often important in obtaining a job or settling in an unfamiliar environment. The goverment legislation which gives preferential treatment to lower castes in some occupations has not been as effective as intended because many people either never assert themselves to take advantage of these opportunities or do not possess even the minimum qualifications required for the occupation. A beginning has been made, however, and it is expected that during the next few years the accessibility of a few higher occupations will set examples and that others will quickly follow suit.

Lower-caste people who work in urban areas but live in the village or maintain active contacts there may become a potent threat to a stratification system based on caste. They are likely to reject openly such traditional criteria of status as caste or family history. They may be able to substitute level of education, occupational status, and income and consumption patterns as relevant criteria for assessing status. Their growing financial independence protects them from economic threats or social boycotts which in the past were effective deterrents. It must be pointed out that it is not probable that they will make planned, concerted efforts to change their social and economic subordination to others. They do not tend to organize themselves as occupational groups, demanding greater representation of their caste in various occupations, but rather to acquiesce to others' efforts from the outside which are generally political in nature.

Although higher castes will be proportionately more represented in higher occupations than lower castes, their traditional monopoly should diminish as lower castes have already started entering such occupations. The less educated among the higher castes may remain farmers or work in small businesses, politics, the police force, or the army. It is expected that as soon as variegated occupational participation becomes a common practice, the division of labor by caste will break down, by the participation of rural labor in nonagricultural occupations, for instance. So far, transportation and construction industries have been absorbing much of the rural labor force. The demand for labor in construction industries, both government and private, fluctuates rapidly, a fact that forces most workers to maintain their economic and social liaison with their villages. Expansion of the government bureaucracies has attracted only those people with some educational qualifications. Only a very small percentage of the rural labor force can expect to enter government bureaucracies or white-collar occupations.

Despite economic uncertainties, urban, industrial and administrative centers will continually attract people of various castes and economic backgrounds. The migrants will carry with them certain elements of rural life. For instance, some may practice caste rules and live in caste-based neighborhoods; this is more likely when migrants retain close contacts with their villages, belong to lower castes, or are employed in lower occupations. Professionals and those high salaried skilled and white-collar workers in government, education, business and industry will mix castes in social contexts without being too concerned about their caste status differences. The development of occupational communities and awareness will form a basis for mutual esteem and status. Identification and participation in caste matters will be limited primarily to marriage and will lead to deviations from endogomy, with the result that caste sanctions will become less severe. All these trends may be anticipated due to the opportunities, constraints and complexities of urban environments.

It is often argued that people in urban and industrial settings will become more caste conscious. The reasons are two-fold — firstly, caste magazines, newspapers and meetings will disseminate information about one's caste-fellows and secondly, greater competition for scarce economic opportunities will increase. Both of these factors will enhance the necessity of organizing, on a caste basis, the sharing of goods and services through political bargaining. It is suggested that the implications of such tactics will not end with limited economic gains, but will stretch to legitimize the caste system itself. The validity of these arguments will depend upon the heterogeneity of various occupational groups. In other words, if persons' caste backgrounds greatly influence the nature of occupational participation, caste-based dwellings, clubs and associations will flourish.

Because lower castes will take a longer time to gain their fair share of higher occupations, caste animosity is likely to be created. The greater the participation of lower castes in various occupations and the greater the development of occupational communities and the awareness of the need for social reform, the more likely it is that caste-consciousness in urban and industrial environments will be a temporary phenomenon.

The recent changes in Indian society have been precipitated by a variety of forces. The interaction between rural and urban environments has set the stage for drastic changes in the stratification system of rural India. Changes in the traditional value system take a long time. A mixture of old and new will form the basis for smooth operation in various institutional areas. Caste has not disappeared, but it does not function as it did in the past. For instance, people of various caste backgrounds work together and share public facilities, but rarely marry outside of their own castes. Also, most people do not care about their caste status in economic and political spheres. It may be inferred that caste will be but a minor aspect of social stratification once other bases of social relations are developed.

Land will continue to be an important source of sustenance, but it will become a less effective basis for exploiting socially depressed groups. More frequent contacts with urban, industrial and administrative centers will make education more valuable. Education will be the most important resource in occupational achievement. The educated will not only be accorded greater esteem, but will also participate in the urban culture more easily. People have begun to understand the growing importance of education to contemporary Indian society. Although education has not always assured people of commensurate occupational participation, rich and poor, higher caste and lower caste are all investing more and more in the education of their children.

Urban occupations will continue to be ranked more highly in the prestige hierarchy than most agricultural occupations. The expectations of better living have been a prime factor in motivating people to accept steady manual occupations in preference to working on a small piece of land which provides considerable independence but limited income. Most people understand that meager landholdings will not be an adequate means of support for growing households unless there are supplementary sources.

The salience of landholding in the future stratification system is difficult to assess. If economic development is slow and population growth does not decline considerably, land may become more valuable than it has ever been in the past. People may consider land a safe investment. Although many people are unable to find jobs other than those connected with agriculture, they are not yet disenchanted with their future possibilities. Landholding, however, is not a viable solution for the majority of people living in rural areas and promises an inadequate means of livelihood for most. Currently, land ownership is an important aspect of the stratification system because income from land is the basis for investments in education. Job opportunities outside agriculture and contact with urban centers will make land somewhat less important in the emerging stratification system.

The prestige of an occupation will be based upon both the education it requires and the amount of income it accrues to its practioner. The economic status of an individual or a family will be evaluated primarily on the basis of income. Since there is a scarcity of land and other property, people will think of upward mobility more in terms of monetary incomes that can provide sustenance than in terms of land ownership. Agriculturists will have occupational titles and their economic status will be judged on the basis of income relative to other occupations. Since occupational prestige is positively associated with education and income it may become the most important dimension of the emerging stratification system. Occupational status will become the institutionalized basis for inequality in both rural and urban areas. It should be added, however, that in rural areas income from land will still be an additional criterion for status distinctions. Although greater similarities between rural and urban stratification will develop, the former will still retain traditional status rewards.

Present trends indicate that an open and achievement-based type of stratification is evolving and that it is in the process of becoming pervasive and institutionalized. Education and occupation will assume more importance than ever before, and the positive relationship between the two is likely to increase. Caste and property status will continue to influence educational and occupational achievement, but such influences will decline when the industrial sector becomes stronger, offering more employment opportunities. The use of scientific methods of cultivation will strengthen the industrial sector and the surplus labor force in agriculture can be employed in diverse industrial occupations. The status system will become freer and and competition will slowly replace the ascriptive routes of higher status. In such a stratification system we expect that education, occupation, and income (instead of inherited land or property) will show higher and more positive associations among themselves. The key, in this system of interrelationships, is education, which prepares the way for lucrative occupations.

Educational and occupational mobility will increase with the expansion of educational facilities and the development of a diversified occupational structure. The family background — with respect to education and occupation — will influence the educational and occupational status of future generations. Such factors as caste and land ownership will become less highly valued. The impact of educational and occupational mobility will contribute to the emergence and institutionalization of a relatively open and competitive stratification system. However, such trends are dependent upon rapid economic growth, which is expected to create a variety of occupational opportunities and make education more valuable. The "green revolution" has made these trends more credible.

We suggest that Indian society is moving towards a system of stratification that is less ascriptive. People will no longer be systematically denied opportunities to compete for higher status. The future of depressed castes and other poor is still in question. Will they be able to overcome the vicious circle of exploitation, poverty and degradation? The answer is not clear, although we have noted some positive trends. Unless some revolutionary attempts are made by the government, not only to provide subsidized educational facilities and preference in occupational recruitment, but also to upgrade the living conditions of the poor, they will predominantly constitute the lower echelons of the stratification system. Concerted political action for preferential treatment of the lower castes in economic spheres has been partially successful, although its impact in leveling off disparities between various groups has yet to be assessed.

(In the final analysis, it seems that the Indian stratification system will become more open; that is to say, education, occupation and income will largely determine a person's general status. The interrelationships among these dimensions will increase, while influence of caste on them will decline. The rural stratification system will resemble the urban stratification system, in which objective dimensions of status will occupy a prominent place in the stratification system. Although numerically and economically dominant groups will have greater access to political power, such groups will become less homogeneous with respect to caste status. The identification of a common goal will be the important criterion in the formation of interest groups.)

Greater geographical mobility, contacts with urban and industrial centers, abolition of legal disabilities, literacy and education, as well as participation in nontraditional occupations will enhance individual mobility. Continued economic growth, accompanied by rapid industrialization and urbanization, greater political participation, and control of the bulk of national resources by democratically elected governments will require that position in the stratification system be based on achievement in relevant contexts. It should be added that general family background and capacity for economic and political bargaining will still influence in complex ways the degree of access to various sources of higher status. The transformation of "caste society" into "open class society" will depend upon the level of economic development and the role of government in the distribution of resources, on the one hand, and on the influence of caste status on educational and occupational achievement on the other. The contemporary trends indicate that the development of an open class society in India has already begun, cutting across caste lines while maintaining its social structural peculiarities. The Indian stratification system will resemble more and more the stratification systems of other industrialized societies.

Bibliography

Alker, Hayward J., and Russett, Bruce M. "On Measuring Inequality". *Behavioral Science* 9 (1969): 207–218.

Arora, Satish K., and Lasswell, Harold D. *Political Communication: The Public Language of Political Elites in India and The United States.* New York: Holt, Rinehart and Winston, Inc., 1969.

Bailey, F. G. *Caste and Economic Frontier: A Village in Highland Orissa.* Manchester: Manchester University Press, 1959.

Bailey, F. G. "Closed Stratification in India." *European Journal of Sociology* 4 (1963): 107–124.

Barber, Bernard. *Social Stratification: A Comparative Analysis of Structure and Process.* New York: Harcourt, Brace and World, Inc., 1957.

Barnabas, A. P., and Mehta, Subhash C. *Caste in Changing India.* New Delhi: Indian Institute of Public Administration, 1965.

Barth, Fredrik. "The System of Social Stratification in Swat, North Pakistan." In *Aspects of Caste in South India, Ceylon and North-West Pakistan,* edited by E. R. Leach, pp. 113–146. London: Cambridge University Press, 1960.

Baum, Rainer C. "On Political Modernity: Stratification and the Generation of Societal Power." In *Perspective on Modernization,* edited by Edward B. Harvey, pp. 22–49. Toronto: University of Toronto Press, 1972.

Beals, Alan R. "Change in the Leadership of a Mysore Village." In *India's Villages,* edited by M. N. Srinivas, pp. 147–160. Bombay: Asia Publishing House, 1955.

Beals, Alan R. "Interplay Among Factors of Change in a Mysore Village." In *Village India: Studies in the Little Community,* edited by McKim Marriott, pp. 78–101. Chicago: The University of Chicago Press, 1955.

Beals, Alan R. *Gopalpur: A South Indian Village.* New York: Holt, Rinehart and Winston, 1962.

Bendix, Reinhard, and Lipset, Seymour M., eds. *Class, Status and Power: A Reader in Social Stratification.* Glencoe, Illinois: The Free Press, 1953.

Bendix, Reinhard, and Lipset, Seymour M., eds. *Class, Status and Power: Social Stratification in Comparative Perspective,* 2d ed. New York: The Free Press, 1966.

Bendix, Reinhard, and Lipset, Seymour M. "Karl Marx's Theory of Social Classes." In *Class, Status and Power: Social Stratification in Comparative Perspective,* 2d ed. edited by Reinhard Bendix and Seymour M. Lipset, pp. 6–11. New York: The Free Press, 1966.

Berreman, Gerald D. "Caste in India and The United States." *American Journal of Sociology* 66 (1960): 120–127.

Berreman, Gerald D. "Caste Racism and Stratification." *Contributions to Indian Sociology* 6 (1962): 122–125.

Berreman, Gerald D. "The Study of Caste Ranking in India." *South Western Journal of Anthropology* 21 (1965): 115–129.

Beteille, Andre. *Caste, Class and Power: Changing Patterns of Stratification in a Tanjore Village.* Berkeley: University of California Press, 1965.

Blau, Peter M., and Duncan, Otis D. *The American Occupational Structure.* New York: John Wiley and Sons Inc., 1967.

Bose, Nirmal K. "Some Aspects of Caste in Bengal." In *Traditional India: Structure and Change,* edited by Milton Singer, pp. 191–206. Philadelphia: The American Folklore Society, 1959.

Bottomore, T. B. *Elites and Society.* New York: Basic Books, 1964.

Bottomore, T. B. *Classes in Modern Society.* New York: Pantheon Books, 1966.

Brown, Norman W. "Class and Cultural Traditions in India." In *Traditional India: Structure and Change,* edited by Milton Singer, pp. 35–39. Philadelphia: The American Folklore Society, 1959.

Carlsson, Gosta. *Social Mobility and Class Structure.* Lund, Sweden: CWK Gleerup, 1958.

Carstairs, G. Morris. "A Village in Rajasthan: A Study in Rapid Social Change." In *India's Villages,* edited by M. N. Srinivas, pp. 36–41. Bombay: Asia Publishing House, 1955.

Chitnis, Suma. "Education for Equality: Case of Scheduled Castes in Higher Education." *Economic and Political Weekly* 7 (1972): 1675–1681.

Cohn, Bernard S. "Changing Tradition of a Low Caste." In *Traditional India: Structure and Change,* edited by Milton Singer, pp. 205–215. Philadelphia: The American Folklore Society, 1957.

Cook, David R. "Prestige of Occupations in India." *Psychological Studies* 7 (1962): 31–37.

Cox, Oliver C. *Caste, Class and Race: A Study in Social Dynamics.* New York: Doubleday Company, Inc., 1948.

Dahrendorf, Ralf. *Class and Class Conflict in Industrial Society.* Stanford: Stanford University Press, 1959.

Damle, Y. B. "Reference Group Theory With Regard to Mobility in Caste." *Social Action* 13 (1963): 190–199.

Davis, Kingsley. *Human Society.* New York: The Macmillan Company, 1948.

Davis, Kingsley. *The Population of India and Pakistan.* Princeton: Princeton University Press, 1951.

Davis, Kingsley, and Moore, Wilbert E. "Some Principles of Stratification." *American Sociological Review* 10 (1945): 242–249.

deReuck, Anthony, and Knight, Julie, eds. *Caste and Race: Comparative Approaches.* London: J. and A. Churchill, Ltd., 1967.

Desai, I. P. "Understanding Occupational Change in India." *Economic and Political Weekly* 6 (1971): 1094–1098.

Deshpande, G. P. "From Caste to Class in Maharashtra." *Economic and Political Weekly* 6 (1971): 485–486.

DeVos, George, and Wagatsuma, Hiroshi, eds. *Japan's Invisible Race: Caste in Culture and Personality.* Berkeley: University of California Press, 1967.

Doreian, Patrick, and Stockman, Norman. "A Critique of the Multi-dimensional Approach to Stratification." *The Sociological Review* 17 (1969): 47–65.

Driver, Edwin D. "Caste and Occupational Structure in Central India." *Social Forces* 41 (1962): 26–31.

D'Souza, Victor A. "Social Grading of Occupations in India." *The Sociological Review* 10 (1962): 145–159.

D'Souza, Victor A. "Social Grading of Village Occupations." *Journal of Gujarat Research Society* 26 (1964): 33–44.

Dube, S. C. *Indian Village.* Ithaca: Cornell University Press, 1955.

Dube, S. C. "A Deccan Village." In *India's Villages,* edited by M. N. Srinivas, pp. 202–215. Bombay: Asia Publishing House, 1955.

Dube, S. C. "Caste Dominance and Factionalism." *Contributions to Indian Sociology* 2 (1968): 58–81.

Dumont, Louis. *Homo Hierarchicus: An Essay on The Caste System.* Chicago: The University of Chicago Press, 1970.

Duncan, Otis D. "Methodological Issues in the Analysis of Social Mobility" In *Social Structure and Mobility in Economic Development,* edited by Neil J. Smelser and Seymour M. Lipset, pp. 51–97. Chicago: Aldine Publishing Company, 1966.

Elder, Joseph W. "Land Consolidation in An Indian Village: A Case Study of the Consolidation of Holdings Act in Uttar Pradesh." *Economic Development and Culture Change* 11 (1962): 16–40.

Floud, Jean. "The Educational Experience of Adult Population of England and Wales as at July 1949." In *Social Mobility in Britain,* edited by D. V. Glass, pp. 98–140. London: Routledge and Kegan Paul, Ltd., 1954.

Freed, Stanley A. "Objective Method of Determining Collective Caste Hierarchy of An Indian Village." *American Anthropologist* 65 (1963): 879–891.

Furer-Haimendorf, Cristoph Von., ed. *Caste and Kin in Nepal, India and Ceylon: Anthropological Studies in Hindu-Buddhist Contact Zones.* Bombay: Asia Publishing House, 1966.

Galanter, Marc. "Law and Caste in Modern India." *Asian Survey* 3 (1963): 544–559.

Gerth, Hans H., and Mills, C. Wright. *From Max Weber: Essays in Sociology.* New York: Oxford University Press, 1958.

Ghurye, G. S. *Caste and Class in India.* Bombay: The Popular Book Depot, 1950.

Gist, Noel P. "Educational Differentials in South India." *Journal of Educational Sociology* 28 (1955): 315–324.

Glass, D. V., ed. *Social Mobility in Britain.* London: Routledge and Kegan Paul Ltd., 1954.

Goode, William J. "Family and Mobility." In *Class, Status and Power: Social Stratification in Comparative Perspective,* 2nd edition, edited by Reinhard Bendix and Seymour M. Lipset, pp. 582–601. New York: The Free Press, 1966.

Gough, Kathleen E. "The Social Structure of a Tanjore Village." In *Village India: Studies in the Little Community,* edited by McKim Marriott, pp. 36–52. Chicago: The University of Chicago Press, 1955.

Gould, Harold A. "Castes, Outcastes, and the Sociology of Stratification." *International Journal of Comparative Sociology* 1 (1960): 220–238.

Gould, Harold A. "Sanskritization and Westernization: A Dynamic View." *The Economic Weekly* 13 (1961): 945–950.

Gould, Harold A. "The Adaptive Functions of Caste in Contemporary Indian Society." *Asian Survey* 3 (1963): 427–438.

Guha, Uma. "Caste Among Rural Bengali Muslims." *Man In India* 45 (1965): 167–169.

Gumperz, John J. "Dialect Differences and Social Stratification in a North Indian Village." *American Anthropologist* 60 (1958): 668–682.

Haller, Archibald O. "Changes in the Structure of Status Systems." *Rural Sociology* 35 (1970): 469–487.

Haller, Archibald O., and Miller, Irwin W. *The Occupational Aspiration Scale.* Cambridge: Schenkman Publishing Company, Inc., 1971.

Harper, Edward B. "Social Consequences of An 'Unsuccessful' Low Caste Movement." In *Social Mobility in the Caste System In India,* edited by James Silverberg, pp. 36–65. The Hague: Mouton Publishers, 1968.

Heller, Celia S., ed. *Structured Social Inequality: A Reader in Comparative Social Stratification,* New York: The Macmillan Company, 1969.

Henderson, A. M., and Parsons, Talcott, eds. *Max Weber: The Theory of Social and Economic Organization.* New York: The Free Press, 1964.

Hitchock, John T. "The Idea of the Martial Rajput." In *Traditional India: Structure and Change,* edited by Milton Singer, pp. 10–17. Philadelphia: The American Folklore Society, 1959.

Hodge, Robert W., and Siegel, Paul M. "The Measurement of Social Class." In *International Encyclopedia of the Social Sciences*, edited by David L. Sills, Vol. 15, pp. 316–325. New York: The Macmillan Company and The Free Press, 1968.

Hodge, Robert W., Treiman, Donald J., and Rossi, Peter H. "A Comparative Study of Occupational Prestige." In *Class, Status and Power: Social Stratification in Comparative Perspective*, 2d ed. edited by Reinhard Bendix and Seymour M. Lipset, pp. 309–321. New York, The Free Press, 1966.

Hoselitz, Bert F. "Interaction Between Industrial and Pre-industrial Stratification Systems." In *Social Structure and Mobility in Economic Development*, edited by Neil J. Smelser and Seymour M. Lipset, pp. 177–193. Chicago: Aldine Publishing Company, 1966.

Huaco, George A. "The Functionalist Theory of Stratification: Two Decades of Controversy." In *Readings on Social Stratification*, edited by Melvin M. Tumin, pp. 411–428. Englewood Cliffs, N.J.: Prentice-Hall, Inc., 1970.

Hutton, J. H. *Caste in India: Its Nature, Function and Origins*. London: Oxford University Press, 1951.

Inkeles, Alex, and Rossi, Peter H. "National Comparisons of Occupational Prestige." *American Journal of Sociology* 61 (1956): 329–339.

Isaacs, Harold R. *India's Ex-untouchables*. New York: The John Day Co., 1965.

Jackson, Elton F. "Status Consistency and Symptoms of Stress." *American Sociological Review* 27 (1962): 469–480.

Kahl, Joseph A. ed. *Comparative Perspective on Stratification: Mexico, Great Britain, Japan*. Boston: Little Brown and Company, 1968.

Kahl, Joseph A., "Introduction." In *Comparative Perspectives on Stratification: Mexico, Great Britain, Japan*, edited by Joseph A. Kahl, pp. ix–xvii. Boston: Little Brown and Company, 1968.

Karve, Irawati. *Hindu Society — An Interpretation*. Poona, India: Deccan College, 1961.

Kivlin, Joseph E., Roy, Prodipto, Fliegel, Frederick C., and Sen, Lalit K. *Communication in India: Experiments in Introducing Change*. Hyderabad, India: National Institute of Community Development, 1968.

Kothari, Rajni, and Maru, Rushikesh. "Caste and Secularism in India: Case Study of Caste Federation." *Journal of Asian Studies* 25 (1965): 33–50.

Krishnan, B. "Social Prestige of Occupations." *Journal of Vocational and Educational Guidance* 3 (1956): 18–32.

Krishnan, B. "Regional Influence on Occupational Preferences." *Psychological Studies* 6 (1961): 66–70.

Lambert, Richard D. "Untouchability as a Social Problem: Theory and Research." *Sociological Bulletin* 7 (1958): 55–61.

Lambert, Richard D. *Workers, Factories and Social Change in India*. Princeton: Princeton University Press, 1963.

Lasswell, Thomas E. *Class and Stratum: An Introduction to Concept and Research*. Boston: Houghton Mifflin Co., 1965.

Lasswell, Thomas E. "Social Stratification: 1964–1968." *Annals of The American Academy of Political and Social Science* 384 (1969): 104–134.

Laumann, Edward O., ed. *Social Stratification: Research and Theory for the 1970's*. Indianapolis: The Bobbs-Merrill Co., Inc., 1970.

Laumann, Edward O., Siegel, Paul M., Hodge Robert W., eds. The *Logic of Social Hierarchies*. Chicago: Markham Publishing Co., 1970.

Leach, E. R., ed. *Aspects of Caste in South India, Ceylon and North-west Pakistan*. London: Cambridge University Press, 1960.

Lenski, Gerhard E. "Status Crystallization: A Non-vertical Dimension of Social Status." *American Sociological Review* 19 (1954): 405–413.

Lenski, Gerhard E. "Social Participation and Status Crystallization." *American Sociological Review* 21 (1956): 458–464.

Lenski, Gerhard E. *Power and Privilege: A Theory of Social Stratification*. New York: McGraw-Hill Book Company, 1966.

Lewis, David M., and Haller, Archibald, O. "Rural-Urban Differences in Pre-industrial and Industrial Evaluations of Occupations by Adolescent Japanese Boys." *Rural Sociology* 29 (1964): 324–329.

Lewis Oscar. *Village Life in Northern India: Studies in a Delhi Village*. Urbana: University of Illinois Press, 1958.

Lipset, Seymour M. "Social Class." In *International Encyclopedia of The Social Sciences*, edited by David L. Sills, Vol. 15, pp. 296–316. New York: The Macmillan Company and The Free Press, 1968 .

Lipset, Seymour M., and Bendix, Reinhard. *Social Mobility in Industrial Society*. Berkeley: University of California Press, 1962.

Mack, Raymond W., ed. *Race, Class and Power*. New York: American Book Company, 1968.

Madan, T. N. "Caste and Development." *Economic and Political Weekly* 4 (1968): 285–290.

Mahar, J. Michael, ed. *The Untouchables in Contemporary India*. Tucson: The University of Arizona Press, 1972.

Mahar, P. M. "A Ritual Pollution Scale for Ranking Hindu Castes." *Sociometry* 23 (1960): 292–306.

Majumdar, D. N. *Caste and Communication in an Indian Village*. Bombay: Asia Publishing House, 1962.

Mandelbaum, David G. "Social Organization and Planned Cultural Change in India." In *India's Villages*, edited by M. N. Srinivas, pp. 15–20. Bombay: Asia Publishing House, 1955.

Mandelbaum, David G. *Status Seeking in Indian Villages*. Reprint No. 270, Center for South Asia Studies and Institute of International Studies. Berkeley: University of California, 1968.

Mandelbaum, David G. *Society in India*. 2 vols. Berkeley: University of California Press, 1970.

Marriott, McKim. "Social Structure and Change in a U. P. Village." In *India's Villages*, edited by M. N. Srinivas, pp. 106–121. Bombay: Asia Publishing House, 1955.

Marriott, McKim, ed. *Village India: Studies in the Little Community*. Chicago: The University of Chicago Press, 1955.

Marriott, McKim. "Caste Ranking and Food Transactions: A Matrix Analysis." In *Structure and Change in Indian Society*, edited by Milton Singer and Bernard Cohn, pp. 133–171. Chicago: Aldine Publishing Company, 1968.

Marriott, McKim. "Multiple Reference in Indian Caste Systems." In *Social Mobility in the Caste System in India*, edited by James Silverberg, pp. 103–114. The Hague: Mouton Publishers, 1968.

Marx, Karl. "On Class." In *Structured Social Inequality: A Reader in Comparative Social Stratification*, edited by Celia S. Heller, pp. 14–24. London: The Macmillan Company, 1969.

Mason, Philip, ed. *India and Ceylon: Unity and Diversity*. London: Oxford University Press, 1967.

Mason, Philip. "Unity and Diversity: An Introductory Review." In *India and Ceylon: Unity and Diversity*, edited by Philip Mason, pp. 1–29. London: Oxford University Press, 1967.

Mathur, K. S. "Caste and Occupation in a Malwa Village." *Eastern Anthropologist* 12 (1958): 47–61.

Mayer, Adrian C. *Caste and Kinship in Central India: A Village and Its Region.* Berkeley: University of California Press, 1960.

Mayer, Adrian C. "Caste and Local Politics in India." In *India and Ceylon: Unity and Diversity,* edited by Philip Mason, pp. 121–141. London: Oxford University Press, 1967.

Mehta, Surinder K. "Patterns of Residence in Poona (India) by Income, Education and Occupation." *American Journal of Sociology* 73 (1968): 496–508.

Metcalf, Thomas. "Landlords Without Land: The U.P. Zamindars Today." *Pacific Affairs* XL (1967): 5–18.

Misra, B. B. *The Indian Middle Classes: Their Growth in Modern Times.* London: Oxford University Press, 1961.

Morris-Jones, W. H. *The Government and Politics in India.* London: Hutchinson University Library, 1964.

Mosca, Gaetano. *The Ruling Class.* New York: McGraw-Hill Book Co., Inc., 1939.

Mukerjee, Radhakamal. "Social Structure and Stratification of the Indian Nation." *Transactions of the Second World Congress of Sociology* 2 (1954): 16–25.

Mukherjee Ramkrishna. "A Further Note on the Analysis of Data on Social Mobility." In *Social Mobility in Britain,* edited by D.V. Glass, pp. 242–259. London: Routledge and Kegan Paul, Ltd., 1954.

Mukherjee, Ramkrishna and Hall, J. R. "A Note on the Analysis of Data on Social Mobility." In *Social Mobility in Britain,* edited by D.V. Glass, pp. 219–239. London: Routledge and Kegan Paul, Ltd., 1954.

Myrdal, Gunnar. *Asian Drama: An Inquiry Into the Poverty of Nations.* New York: Random House, 1968.

Nair, Kusum. *Blossoms in the Dust: The Human Factors in Indian Development.* New York: Frederick A. Praeger, 1961.

National Institute of Community Development. *Diffusion of Innovations in Rural Societies — India Phase II Codes.* Hyderabad, India: National Institute of Community Development, 1968.

Neale, Walter C. *Economic Change in Rural India: Land Tenure and Reform in Uttar Pradesh, 1800–1955.* New Haven: Yale University Press, 1962.

Nijhawan, N. K. "Occupational Mobility and Political Development: Some Preliminary Findings." *Economic and Political Weekly* 6 (1971): 317–324.

Olcott, Mason. "The Caste System of India." *American Sociological Review* 9 (1944): 648–657.

Opler, Morris E., and Singh, Rudra Datt. "Two Villages of Eastern Uttar Pradesh (U.P.), India: An Analysis of Similarities and Differences." *American Anthropologist* 54 (1952): 179–190.

Parsons, Talcott. "A Revised Analytical Approach to the Theory of Social Stratification." In *Class, Status and Power: A Reader in Social Stratification,* edited by Reinhard Bendix and Seymour M. Lipset, pp. 92–128. Glencoe, Illinois: The Free Press, 1953.

Parsons, Talcott. "Equality and Inequality in Modern Society, or Social Stratification Revisited." In *Social Stratification: Research and Theory for the 1970's,* edited by Edward O. Laumann, pp. 13–72. Indianapolis: The Bobbs-Merrill Company, Inc., 1970.

Paulus, Caleb R. "A Study of Social Stratification in Banglore City." *Pacific Sociological Review* 11 (1968): 49–56.

Porter, John. *The Vertical Mosaic: An Analysis of Social Class and Power In Canada.* Toronto: University of Toronto Press, 1965.

Rao, M. S. A. "Caste and the Indian Army." *Economic Weekly* 13 (1964): 1439–1443.

Redfield, Robert, and Singer, Milton. "Foreword." In *Village India: Studies in The*

Little Community, edited by McKim Marriott, pp. vii–xvi. Chicago: The University of Chicago Press, 1955.

Reissman, Leonard. "Class and Power: The Sacred and the Profane." *Views* 6 (1964): 46–51.

Reissman, Leonard. "Social Stratification." *In Sociology*, edited by Neal J. Smelser, pp. 206–268. New York: John Wiley and Sons, Inc., 1967.

Robins, Robert S. "India: Judicial Panchayats in Uttar Pradesh." *American Journal of Comparative Law* 11 (1962): 239–246.

Robins, Robert S. "Political Elite Formation in Rural India: The Uttar Pradesh Panchayat Elections of 1949, 1956, and 1961." *Journal of Politics* 29 (1967): 838–860.

Rosen, George. *Democracy and Economic Change in India*. Berkeley: University of California Press, 1967.

Rowe, W. L. "Changing Rural Class Structure and the Jajmani System." *Human Organization* 22 (1963): 41–44.

Roy, Prodipto, Fliegel, Frederick C., Kivlin, Joseph E., and Sen, Lalit K. *Agricultural Innovation Among Indian Farmers*. Hyderabad, India: National Institute of Community Development, 1968.

Rudolph, Lloyd I. "The Modernity of Traditions: The Democratic Incarnation of Castes in India." *American Political Science Review* 59 (1965): 975–989.

Rudolph, Lloyd I., and Rudolph, Susanne H. *The Modernity of Tradition: Political Development in India*. Chicago: University of Chicago Press, 1967.

Sarma, Jyotirmoyee. "A Village in West Bengal." In *India's Villages*, edited by M. N. Srinivas, pp. 180–201. Bombay: Asia Publishing House, 1955.

Schwartz, Barton M., ed. *Caste in Overseas Indian Communities*. San Francisco: Chandler Publishing Company, 1967.

Sen, Lalit K., and Roy, Prodipto. *Awareness of Community Development in Village India: Preliminary Report*. Hyderabad, India: National Institute of Community Development, 1966.

Shah, A. M., and Shroff, R. G. "The Vahivanca Barots of Gujarat: A Caste of Genealogists and Mythographers." In *Traditional India: Structure and Change*, edited by Milton Singer, pp. 40–70. Philadelphia: American Folklore Society, 1959.

Sharma, Kailas N. "Occupational Mobility of Castes in a North Indian Village." *South-Western Journal of Anthropology* 17 (1961): 146–164.

Silverberg, James, ed. *Social Mobility in the Caste System in India*. The Hague: Mouton Publishers, 1968.

Singer, Milton, ed. *Traditional India: Structure and Change*. Philadelphia: The American Folklore Society, 1959.

Singer, Milton, and Cohn, Bernard S. eds. *Structure and Change in Indian Society*. Chicago: Aldine Publishing Company, 1968.

Singh, Baljit, and Misra, Shridhar. *A Study of Land Reforms in Uttar Pradesh*. Calcutta: Oxford Book Company, 1964.

Singh, Harijinder. "Social Grading of Caste and Occupations in an Indian Village." *The Indian Journal of Social Work* 27. (1967): 381–386.

Singh, Indra P., and Harit, H. L. "Effects of Urbanization in a Delhi Suburban Village." *Journal of Social Research* 3 (1960): 38–43.

Singh, K. K. *Patterns of Caste Tension: A Study of Intercaste Tension and Conflict*. Bombay: Asia Publishing House, 1967.

Singh, Vijai P. *Bharat Men Samudayek Vikas* (Community Development in India). Allahabad, India: Ramnarainlall Beniprasad Publishers and Booksellers, 1965.

Singh, Vijai P. "Problems of Theorizing in Empirical Research: The Case of Political Participation Studies." In *Basic Issues in Social Sciences*, edited by K. D. Sharma, pp. 151–160. Bombay: The Academic Journals of India, 1968.

Singh, Vijai P. "The Evolution of a Rural Stratification in India (1930–65)." Ph.D. dissertation. University of Wisconsin, Madison, 1970.

Singh, Vijai P. "Legal Perceptions and Usages in North Indian Village Disputes." Paper read at the American Political Science Association meeting. September 5–9, 1972, at Washington, D.C. Mimeographed.

Singh, Vijai P. "Unity in Diversity: The Dynamics of Ethnic Relations in South Asia." In *Ethnicity in Asian Countries*, edited by T. S. Kang. Buffalo: State University of New York, in press.

Singh, Yogendra. "Group Status of Factions in Rural Community." *Journal of Social Sciences* 2 (1959): 57–67.

Sinha, Surajit. "Status Formation and Rajput Myth in Tribal Central India." *Man in India* 42 (1962): 35–80.

Sivertsen, Dogfinn. *When Caste Barriers Fall: A Study of Social and Economic Changes in a South Indian Village*. New York: Humanities Press, 1963.

Smelser, Neil J., and Lipset, Seymour M., eds. *Social Structure and Mobility in Economic Development*. Chicago: Aldine Publishing Company, 1966.

Smelser, Neil J., and Lipset, Seymour M. "Social Structure, Mobility and Development." In *Social Structure and Mobility in Economic Development*, edited by Neil J. Smelser and Seymour M. Lipset, pp. 1–50. Chicago: Aldine Publishing Company, 1966.

Smith, Donald Eugene. *India as a Secular State*. Princeton: Princeton University Press, 1963.

Smith, Michael. "Pre-industrial Stratification System." In *Social Structure and Mobility in Economic Development*, edited by Neil J. Smelser and Seymour M. Lipset, pp. 141–176. Chicago: Aldine Publishing Company, 1966.

Sorokin, Pitirim. *Social Mobility*. New York: Harper and Row, 1927.

Sorokin, Pitirim. "Social Mobility." In *Structured Social Inequality: A Reader in Comparative Stratification*, edited by Celia S. Heller, pp. 317–325. New York: The Macmillan Company, 1969.

Sovani, N. V., and Pradhan, Kusum. "Occupational Mobility in Poona City Between Three Generations." *Indian Economic Review* 2 (1955): 23–36.

Srinivas, M. N. "The Social System of a Mysore Village." In *Village India: Studies in the Little Community*, edited by McKim Marriott, pp. 1–35. Chicago: The University of Chicago Press, 1955.

Srinivas, M. N., ed. *India's Villages*. Bombay: Asia Publishing House, 1955.

Srinivas, M. N. "A Note on Sanskritization and Westernization." *Far Eastern Quarterly* 15 (1956): 481–496.

Srinivas, M. N. "The Dominant Caste in Rampura." *American Anthropologist* 61 (1959): 1–16.

Srinivas, M. N. *Caste in Modern India and Other Essays*. Bombay: Asia Publishing House, 1962.

Srinivas, M. N. *Social Change in Modern India*. Berkeley: University of California Press, 1969.

Stern, Claudio and Kahl, Joseph A. "Stratification Since the Revolution." In *Comparative Perspective on Stratification: Mexico, Great Britain, Japan*, edited by Joseph A. Kahl, pp. 5–30. Boston: Little Brown and Company, 1968.

Stevenson, H. N. L. "Status Evaluation in the Hindu Caste System." *Journal of Royal Anthropological Institute* 84 (1954): 45–65.

Stinchcombe, Arthur L. "Some Empirical Consequences of the Davis-Moore Theory of Stratification." In *Class, Status and Power: Social Stratification in Comparative Perspective*, 2d ed., edited by Reinhard Bendix and Seymour M. Lipset, pp. 69–72. New York: The Free Press, 1966.

Stinchcombe, Arthur L. "The Structure of Stratification Systems." In *International Encyclopedia of Social Sciences*, Vol. 15, edited by David L. Sills, pp. 325–332. New York: The Macmillan Company and The Free Press, 1968.

Svalastoga, Karre. *Social Differentiation*. New York: David McKay Company, Inc., 1965.

Thielbar, Gerald W., and Feldman, Saul D., eds. *Issues in Social Inequality*. Boston: Little Brown and Company, 1972.

Tumin, Melvin M. "Some Principles of Stratification: A Critical Analysis." *American Sociological Review* 18 (1953): 387–394.

Tumin, Melvin M. *Social Stratification: The Forms and Functions of Inequality*. Englewood Cliffs, N.J.: Prentice-Hall, Inc. 1967.

Tumin, Melvin M., ed. *Readings on Social Stratification*. Englewood Cliffs. N.J.: Prentice-Hall, Inc., 1970.

Tumin, Melvin M., and Feldman, Arnold S. "Theory and Measurement of Occupational Mobility." *American Sociological Review* 22 (1957): 281–292.

Verba, Sidney, Ahmed, B., and Bhatt, A. *Caste, Race and Politics: A Comparative Study of India and United States*. Beverly Hills: Sage Publications, 1971.

Vidyarthi, Lalita P. "Some Preliminary Observations on Inter-group Conflict in India: Tribal, Rural and Industrial." *Journal of Social Research* 10 (1967): 1–10.

Warner, W. Lloyd, Meeker, Marcia, and Eells, Kenneth. *Social Class in America: A Manual of Procedure for the Measurement of Social Status*. Chicago: Science Research Associates, Inc., 1949.

Weber, Max. *The Religion of India*. Glencoe, Illinois: The Free Press, 1958.

Weiner, Myron. *The Politics of Scarcity: Public Pressure and Political Response in India*. Chicago: The University of Chicago Press, 1962.

Wesotowski, Wtodzimierz. "Some Notes on the Functional Theory of Stratification." In *Class, Status and Power: Social Stratification in Comparative Perspective*, 2d ed., edited by Reinhard Bendix and Seymour M. Lipset, pp. 64–69. New York: The Free Press.

Wiser, W. H. *The Hindu Jajmani System*. Lucknow, India: Lucknow Publishing House, 1958.

Wiser, W. H., and Wiser, C. V. *Behind Mud Walls 1930–1960*. Berkeley: University of California Press, 1967.

Wrong, Dennis H. "The Functional Theory of Stratification: Some Neglected Considerations." *American Sociological Review* 24 (1959): 772–782.

Yasuda, Saburo. "A Methodological Inquiry into Social Mobility." *American Sociological Review* 29 (1964): 16–23.

Appendix A

Intercorrelations Among Family Possessions in the Three Villages

Table A–1

INTERCORRELATIONS AMONG IMPORTANT FAMILY POSSESSIONS IN JAITI								
	1	2	3	4	5	6	7	8
1. Land	—	.45	.24	.30	−.15	−.02	.51	.23
2. Bullocks		—	.24	.21	−.01	−.07	.42	.15
3. Cows			—	.13	.00	−.05	.22	.40
4. Buffaloes				—	−.01	−.04	.38	.31
5. Sheep and Goats					—	−.05	−.10	.00
6. Pigs						—	−.07	−.03
7. Bullock Carts							—	.26
8. Chaff cutters								—

Table A–2

INTERCORRELATIONS AMONG IMPORTANT FAMILY POSSESSIONS IN RATU							
	1	2	3	4	5	6	7
1. Land	—	.07	.07	.18	.20	.03	.05
2. Bullocks		—	.31	.05	.09	.03	.00
3. Cows			—	−.24	−.02	−.03	−.11
4. Buffaloes				—	.02	.43	.59
5. Sheep and Goats					—	−.07	−.05
6. Bullock Carts						—	.40
7. Chaff Cutters							—

Table A–3

INTERCORRELATIONS AMONG IMPORTANT FAMILY POSSESSIONS IN BHAGU							
	1	2	3	4	5	6	7
1. Land	—	.49	.05	.43	.00	.41	.51
2. Bullocks		—	.16	.22	.11	.23	.30
3. Cows			—	−.16	−.07	.05	.00
4. Buffaloes				—	.17	−.02	.23
5. Sheep and Goats					—	−.02	−.07
6. Pigs						—	.30
7. Bullock Carts							—

Appendix B

Distributions of Occupations Across Generations in the Three Villages

Table B–1

DISTRIBUTION OF OCCUPATIONS (FROM HIGH TO LOW) ACROSS THREE GENERATIONS IN JAITI

Occupations	Fathers of Respondents	Respondents	Sons of Respondents
Professional, business, and related	4	1	3
Teacher	—	—	2
Clerical and related	—	—	—
Service (Class IV and police)	4	11	7
Skilled worker	27	25	6
Unskilled nonagricultural laborer	—	—	1
Farmer	157	161	32
Agricultural laborer	12	20	—
No information	20	6	1
Total	224	224	52

Table B–2

DISTRIBUTION OF OCCUPATIONS (FROM HIGH TO LOW)
ACROSS THREE GENERATIONS IN RATU

Occupations	Fathers of Respondents	Respondents	Sons of Respondents
Professional, business, and related	—	—	1
Teacher	—	—	—
Clerical and related	—	1	2
Service (Class IV and police)	3	4	2
Skilled worker	9	9	3
Unskilled nonagricultural laborer	—	1	—
Farmer	46	50	10
Agricultural laborer	5	6	4
No information	8	—	—
Total	71	71	22

Table B–3

DISTRIBUTION OF OCCUPATIONS (FROM HIGH TO LOW)
ACROSS THREE GENERATIONS IN BHAGU

Occupations	Fathers of Respondents	Respondents	Sons of Respondents
Professional, business, and related	—	—	1
Teacher	—	—	—
Clerical and related	—	—	—
Service (Class IV and police)	—	2	—
Skilled worker	—	2	—
Unskilled nonagricultural laborer	—	—	—
Farmer	67	77	16
Agricultural laborer	—	1	—
No information	17	2	1
Total	84	84	18

Appendix C

Intercorrelations Among the Stratification
Variables Over the Three Generations

Table C-1

INTERCORRELATIONS AMONG STRATIFICATION VARIABLES FOR FATHERS OF
RESPONDENTS IN JAITI (RESPONDENTS 35–60 YEARS)

	1	2	3	4
1. Caste	—	.30	.55	.22
2. Land		—	.40	.05
3. Education			—	.29
4. Occupation				—

Table C–2

INTERCORRELATIONS AMONG STRATIFICATION VARIABLES FOR
RESPONDENTS IN JAITI (RESPONDENTS 35–60 YEARS)

	1	2	3	4
1. Caste	—	.32	.55	.27
2. Land		—	.41	−.19
3. Education			—	.22
4. Occupation				—

Table C–3

INTERCORRELATIONS AMONG STRATIFICATION VARIABLES FOR SONS OF
RESPONDENTS IN JAITI (RESPONDENTS 35–60 YEARS)

	1	2	3	4
1. Caste	—	.38	.81	.67
2. Land		—	.36	.12
3. Education			—	.71
4. Occupation				—

Table C–4

INTERCORRELATIONS AMONG STRATIFICATION VARIABLES FOR FATHERS OF RESPONDENTS IN RATU (RESPONDENTS 35–60 YEARS)

	1	2	3	4
1. Caste	—	.66	.46	.19
2. Land		—	.54	.10
3. Education			—	.25
4. Occupation				—

Table C–5

INTERCORRELATIONS AMONG STRATIFICATION VARIABLES FOR RESPONDENTS IN RATU (RESPONDENTS 35–60 YEARS)

	1	2	3	4
1. Caste	—	.68	.38	–.01
2. Land		—	.36	.01
3. Education			—	.26
4. Occupation				—

Table C–6

INTERCORRELATIONS AMONG STRATIFICATION VARIABLES FOR SONS OF RESPONDENTS IN RATU (RESPONDENTS 35–60 YEARS)

	1	2	3	4
1. Caste	—	.62	.81	.55
2. Land		—	.43	.60
3. Education			—	.65
4. Occupation				—

Table C-7

INTERCORRELATIONS AMONG STRATIFICATION VARIABLES FOR FATHERS OF
RESPONDENTS IN BHAGU (RESPONDENTS 35–60 YEARS)

	1	2	3	4
1. Caste	—	.09	.13	.00
2. Land		—	.45	.00
3. Education			—	.00
4. Occupation				—

Table C–8

INTERCORRELATIONS AMONG STRATIFICATION VARIABLES FOR
RESPONDENTS IN BHAGU (RESPONDENTS 35–60 YEARS)

	1	2	3	4
1. Caste	—	.13	−.08	−.15
2. Land		—	.13	−.22
3. Education			—	.29
4. Occupation				—

Table C–9

INTERCORRELATIONS AMONG STRATIFICATION VARIABLES FOR SONS OF
RESPONDENTS IN BHAGU (RESPONDENTS 35–60 YEARS)

	1	2	3	4
1. Caste	—	−.40	−.21	−.07
2. Land		—	.66	.19
3. Education			—	−.16
4. Occupation				—

Table C–10

INTERCORRELATIONS AMONG STRATIFICATION VARIABLES FOR FATHERS OF
RESPONDENTS OF THREE COMMUNITIES (RESPONDENTS 35–60 YEARS)

	1	2	3	4
1. Caste	—	.30	.51	.23
2. Land		—	.42	.05
3. Education			—	.29
4. Occupation				—

Table C–11

INTERCORRELATIONS AMONG STRATIFICATION VARIABLES FOR
RESPONDENTS OF THREE COMMUNITIES (RESPONDENTS 35–60 YEARS)

	1	2	3	4
1. Caste	—	.32	.48	.18
2. Land		—	.36	–.15
3. Education			—	.24
4. Occupation				—

Table C–12

INTERCORRELATIONS AMONG STRATIFICATION VARIABLES FOR SONS OF
RESPONDENTS OF THREE COMMUNITIES (RESPONDENTS 35–60 YEARS)

	1	2	3	4
1. Caste	—	.35	.67	.65
2. Land		—	.41	.21
3. Education			—	.64
4. Occupation				—

Table C–13

INTERCORRELATIONS AMONG STRATIFICATION VARIABLES FOR FATHERS OF
RESPONDENTS OF THREE COMMUNITIES (ALL CASES)

	1	2	3	4
1. Caste	—	.29	.44	.26
2. Land		—	.33	.08
3. Education			—	.23
4. Occupation				—

Table C–14

INTERCORRELATIONS AMONG STRATIFICATION VARIABLES FOR
RESPONDENTS OF THREE COMMUNITIES (ALL CASES)

	1	2	3	4
1. Caste	—	.29	.45	.21
2. Land		—	.28	–.12
3. Education			—	.20
4. Occupation				—

Table C–15

INTERCORRELATIONS AMONG STRATIFICATION VARIABLES FOR SONS OF
RESPONDENTS OF THREE COMMUNITIES (ALL CASES)

	1	2	3	4
1. Caste	—	.35	.58	.59
2. Land		—	.42	.22
3. Education			—	.60
4. Occupation				—

Subject Index

A

Achievement
  as basis of inequality, 9
  in emerging stratification system, 121
Age, lack of records of, 98
Ascription
  as basis of inequality, 9
  in emerging stratification system, 112,
    121, 134
  mobility and, 12-13

B

Bourgeoisie, 4
Brahmins, 21
  declining influence of, 28
  definition of ritual status by, 76
  emulation of, 23

C

Caste(s). *See also* Specific castes
  class and, 31-35
  criteria determining status of, 22-23
  declining importance of, 132
  definition of, 21
  Dominant, 24-25
  numerically dominant, 123
  occupation and, 25-26
  as status groups, 7
  as unit of analysis, 40-42
Caste communities, 128
Caste consciousness, urban, 131-132
Caste councils, 77
Caste identity, weakening, 128-129
Caste inequality
  during 1930-46, 75-77
  during 1947-65, 77-80
Caste solidarity, 41
Caste status
  interactional ranking of, 52
  occupational mobility and, 107-108
  ranking of, 51-57
  reputational ranking of, 52
  stratification and, 44-45
Caste stratification, 21-23
Caste system
  changes in, 30-31, 123
  mobility in, 23-25, 27-29
Caste taboos, punishment for violation
  of, 76
Ceremonies, caste inequalities and, 76,
  77-78
Changes in stratification, 121-135
  theoretical approaches to, 122
Cities, migration to, 125-126, 130
Class, *See also* Social class
Class consciousness, in Marxian theory,
  5
Closed stratification systems, 9
  mobility in, 12
  permeability in, 14
Community Development programs, 39
  economic inequality and, 82
Community influentials
  characteristics of, 109-111
  identification of, 113, 116
  membership in, 112, 116-117
Cooperative societies, 85, 123

D

Data sources, 43-47
Dominance, numerical, 123
Dominant Caste, 24-25
Dress, caste inequality and, 78

E

Economic growth, mobility and, 12-13
Economic inequality, 80
   changes in, 82
Economic status
   access to education and, 129-130
   mobility and, 27-29
Education. *See also* Schools
   comparison of levels of, 45
   increasing, 129
   rising importance of, 132
   value placed on, 104, 127
Educational inequality, 87
   changes in, 87-88
Educational mobility, 99, 100-104, 108
   in emerging stratification system,
      133-134
Educational status
   definition of, 66
   measurement of, 66-67
   occupation related to, 66
Elections. *See also* Franchise
   for panchayats, 82, 84
Employment. *See also* Occupation(s)
   mobility and, 33
   in urban areas, 125-127, 130-131, 132

F

Family
   definition of, 42
   importance in caste system, 42
Farmers, definition and status of, 68
Franchise
   effect on political power, 64, 124
   influence on stratification, 30

G

Greetings, caste inequality and, 78

H

Hindus, caste status of, 52
Honor, social estimation of, 6
Horizontal mobility, 12
Housing patterns, caste and, 75, 78

I

Income, occupational prestige and, 133
Indian stratification
   caste status and, 44-45
   dimensions of, 27-29, 51
   dominant caste and, 24-25
   emerging system of, 121-135
   external forces acting on, 29-31

Indian stratification (**Continued**)
   intergenerational correlations among
      dimensions of, 90-97
   ritual status, 21-23
   Sanskritization and, 23-24, 124
   study of, 16
   Westernization and, 24, 124
Inequality. *See also* Caste inequality;
      Economic inequality; Educational
      inequality; Occupational inequality
   definition of, 43
   functionalist concept of, 8-9
Interactional ranking, 52
Interaction patterns
   caste and, 75, 78, 79-80
   rural-urban, 126
Intergenerational mobility, 12
   educational, 99, 100-104, 108
   Occupational, 99, 105-108
   problems in study of, 13

K

Kshatriyas, 21
   ritual status of, 76

L

Landholding. *See also* Zamindari system
   in emerging stratification system,
      126, 132-133
   inequality in, 80
   as measure of property status, 59-63
   occupational mobility and, 107
Landlords. *See also* Zamindari system
   power of, 32-34
Land reform legislation, 36-37
   effect on class, 32-33
Leadership. *See also* Political power
   bases of, 16, 45
   changes in, 99
Literacy, 66, 129
Livestock, caste status related to, 60

M

Mobility. *See also* Educational mobility;
      Intergenerational mobility;
      Occupational mobility; Social mo-
      bility
Muslims, caste status of, 52

N

Nyay panchayats, 35, 84-85

O

Occupation(s). *See also* Employment
  caste and, 25-26, 76
  defiling, 124-125
  educational status related to, 66
  as index of stratification, 3-4
  saleable, 126-127
Occupational communities, 128-129
  caste consciousness and, 132
Occupational inequality, 76, 87
  changes in, 88
Occupational levels, comparison of, 45
Occupational mobility, 99, 105-108
  in emerging stratification system, 133-134
  problems in study of, 13
Occupational status
  definition of, 68
  in emerging stratification system, 132, 133
  ranking of, 68-71
  as stratification dimension, 15
Occupational structure, definition and measurement of, 69-70
Open stratification systems, 9
  mobility in, 12
  permeability in, 14

P

Panchayats, 35-36
  changes in political power and, 89
  elections for, 64
  purposes of, 38-39
  size of, 65
Permeability of social systems, 14-15
Police, involvement in disputes, 81, 82
Political power
  changes in, 82-87, 89, 123
  class definition on basis of, 32
  definition of, 63
  inequality in, 81-82
  measurement of, 63-65
  mobility and, 27-29
Pollution, 21, 22
  declining importance of, 30, 57
Power. *See also* Political power
  class definition on basis of, 34-35
  functionalist concept of, 9-10
  Marxian concept of, 5
Power structure, 64-65
Proletariat, 4
Property. *See also* Landholding
  as basis of stratification, 4-6, 32-33
  family ownership of, 42
Property status, assessment of, 59-63
Punishment, for caste taboo violation, 76
Purity, 21, 22

R

Religion, caste status and, 52
Reputational ranking, 52
Residential patterns, caste inequality and, 75, 78
Revolution, industrialization and, 5-6

S

Sanskritization, 23-24
  failure as means of improving status, 124
Schools
  accessibility of, 95-96
  caste inequality in, 76
Sentiments, caste mobility and, 31
Skilled labor, demand for, 126-127
Social change, mobility and, 12
Social class
  caste and, 31-35
  definition of, 14, 34
  differentiation from stratification, 14
  Marxian concept of, 4-6
  problems in study of, 15-16
  Weberian concept of, 6-7
Social mobility, 123
  within castes, 41-42
  in caste system, 23-25, 27-29
  definition of, 12
  Sanskritization and, 23-24, 124
  stratification dimensions affecting, 12-13
  Westernization and, 24, 124
Social stratification. *See also* Indian stratification
  bases of, 3-4
  conflict theories of, 4-7, 10, 14
  definition of, 11-12, 44
  differentiation from class, 14
  dimensions of, 3-4, 11
  functional theory of, 7-10, 14
  synthesis theory of, 10-11
Social structure, 71
  complexity of, 58
  educational mobility and, 104
  occupational mobility and, 107-108
Status consistency, 117. *See also* Status inconsistency
Status groups, Weberian concept of, 6-7
Status honor, 6

Status inconsistency
  definition of, 12
  in emerging stratification system,
    117-119
  traditional, 117
Stratification. See also Indian stratification; Social stratification
Sudras, 21

T
Two-class system, 34, 35, 109-117

U
Untouchables, 21

V
Vaisyas, 21
Varna system, 21, 22
Vertical mobility, 12
Village panchayats, 35-36, 123
  changes in political power and, 82-86
Villages, selection for study, 38-40
Voting. *See also* Franchise

W
Westernization, as means of improving
  status, 24, 124

Z
Zamindari system, 36, 80
  abolition of, 36-37, 89
  economic controls and, 63
  political power and, 65, 80-81, 88

Author Index

Numbers in *italics* indicate complete refereces.

A

Ahmed, B., *144*
Alker, Hayward J., *136*
Arora, Satish K., *136*

B

Bailey, F. G., 27-28, *49*, 50, *136*
Barber, Bernard, 5, 17, 41, *47*, 48, 50, *136*
Barnabas A, P., *72*, *136*
Barth, Fredrik, *48*, *136*
Baum, Rainer C., *18*, *136*
Beals, Alan R., 26, 28, *48*, 49, *72*, *136*
Bendix, Reinhard, 5, *17*, *136*, *140*
Berreman, Gerald D., *72*, *136*
Beteille, Andre, 26, 28, 32, *48*, 49, *72*, *136*
Bhatt, A., *144*
Blau, Peter M., 13, *16*, 19, *136*
Bose, Nirmal K., *49*, *137*
Bottomore, T. B., *137*
Brown, Norman W., *137*

C

Carlsson, Gosta, *137*
Carstairs, G. Morris, *49*, *137*
Chitnis, Suma, *137*
Cohn, Bernard C., *49*, *137*
Cohn, Bernard S., *142*
Cook, David R., *72*, *137*
Cox, Oliver C., *47*, *137*

D

Dahrendorf, Ralf, 5, *17*, *137*
Damle, Y. B., *137*
Davis, Kingsley, 7-8, 9, *17*, *18*, 23, 48, *137*
de Reuck, Anthony, *137*
Desai, I. P., *137*
Deshpande, G. P., *137*
DeVos, George, *137*
Doreian, Patrick, *137*
Driver, Edwin D., *72*, *137*

D'Souza, Victor S., *72*, *137*
Dube, S. C., 24, 25-26, 29, *48*, 49, 50, 72, *137*
Dumont, Louis, *47*, 48, *137*
Duncan, Otis D., 13, *16*, 19, *136*, *138*

E

Eells, Kenneth, *144*
Elder, Joseph W., 37, *50*, *138*

F

Feldman, Arnold S., *19*, *144*
Feldman, Saul D., *144*
Fliegel, Frederick C., *139*, *142*
Floud, Jean, *19*, *138*
Freed, Stanley A., 52, *72*, *138*
Furer-Haimendorf, Cristoph Von, *138*

G

Galanter, Marc, *138*
Gerth, Hans H., *17*, *18*, *48*, *72*, *138*
Ghurye, G. S., *138*
Gist, Noel P., *138*
Glass, D. V., *138*
Goode, William J., *50*, *138*
Gough, Kathleen E., 28, *49*, *138*
Gould, Harold A., 22, *48*, *138*
Guha, Uma, *138*
Gumperz, John J., *138*

H

Hall, J. R., *141*
Haller, Archibald O., *17*, *138*, *140*
Harit, H. L., *142*
Harper, Edward B., *48*, *72*, *138*
Heller, Celia S., 5, *17*, *138*
Henderson, A. M., *17*, *138*
Hitchcock, John T., 26, *49*, *138*
Hodge, Robert W., *17*, *19*, *139*
Hoselitz, Bert F., *16*, *139*
Huaco, George A., 9-10, 18, *139*
Hutton, J. H., *47*, *139*

I

Inkeles, Alex, *17*, *139*
Isaacs, Harold R., *139*

J

Jackson, Elton F., *18*, *139*

K

Kahl, Joseph A., *16-17*, *18*, *139*, *143*
Karve, Irawati, *47*, 48, *139*
Kivlin, Joseph E., *139*, *142*
Knight, Julie, *137*
Kothari, Rajni, *139*
Krishnan, B., *72*, *139*

L

Lambert, Richard D., *139*
Lasswell, Harold D., *136*
Lasswell, Thomas E., *17*, *18*, 19, *139*
Laumann, Edward O., *139*
Leach, E. R., *139*
Lenski, Gerhard E., 4, 10-11, *17*, *18*, 19, 34, *49*, *139*, *140*
Lewis, David M., *17*, *140*
Lewis, Oscar, *49*, *140*
Lipset, Seymour M., 5, *16*, *19*, *136*, **140**, *143*

Lewis, David M., *17*, *140*
Lewis, Oscar, *49*, *140*
Lipset, Seymour M., 5, *16*, *19*, *136*, *14J*, *143*

M

Mack, Raymond W., *140*
Madan, T. N., *140*
Mahar, J. Michael, *14J*
Mahar, J. Michael, *140*
Majumdar, D. N., 29, *49*, *140*
Mandelbaum, David G., 23-24, 27, *48*, 49, *72*, *140*
Marriott, McKim, 27, 41, *48*, *49*, 50, *71*, *72*, *140*
Maru Rushikesh, *139*
Marx, Karl, 4-6, *17*, *140*
Mason, Philip, 31, *49*, *72*, *140*
Mathur, K. S., *140*
Mayer, Adrian C., 27, *48*, 49, 50, *72*, *141*
Meeker, Marcia, *144*
Mehta, Subhash C., *72*, *136*
Mehta, Surinder K., *141*
Metcalf, Thomas, *50*, *141*

Miller, Irwin W., *138*
Mills, C. Wright, *17*, 18, *48*, *72*, *138*
Misra, B. B., *141*
Misra, Shridhar, *49*, *142*
Moore, Wilbert E., 7-8, *17*, *137*
Morris-Jones, W. H., *141*
Mosca, Gaetano, 34, *49*, *141*
Mukerjee, Radhakamal, *141*
Mukherjee, Ramkrishna, *141*
Myrdal, Gunnar, *141*

N

Nair, Kusum, *141*
National Institute of Community Development, *73*, *141*
Neale, Walter C., *141*
Nijhawan, N. K., *141*

O

Olcott, Mason, *141*
Opler, Morris E., *141*

P

Parsons, Talcott, 8, 9, *17*, *18*, *138*, *141*
Paulus, Caleb R., *141*
Porter, John, 9, *18*, *141*
Pradhan, Kusum, *143*

R

Rao, M. S. A., *141*
Redfield, Robert, *141-142*
Reissman, Leonard, *142*
Robins, Robert S., *49*, *142*
Rosen, George, 32, *49*, *142*
Rossi, Peter H., *17*, *139*
Rowe, W. L., *142*
Roy, Prodipto, *139*, *142*
Rudolph, Lloyd I., *142*
Rudolph, Susanne H., *142*
Russett, Bruce M., *136*

S

Sarma, Jyotirmoyee, 28-29, 49, *142*
Schwartz, Barton M., *142*
Sen, Lalit K., *139*, *142*
Shah, A. M., 26, *49*, *142*
Sharma, Kailas N., *142*
Shroff, R. G., 26, *49*, *142*
Siegel, Paul M., *19*, *139*
Silverberg, James, *142*
Singer, Milton, *141-142*
Singh, Baljit, *49*, *142*
Singh, Harijinder, *142*

Singh, Indra P., *142*
Singh, K. K., 29, *49, 142*
Singh, Rudra Datt, *141*
Singh, Vijai P., *142, 143*
Singh, Yogendra, *143*
Sinha, Surajit, *143*
Sivertsen, Dogfinn, 26, 28-29, *48,* 49, *72, 143*
Smelser, Neil J., *16, 19, 143*
Smith, Donald Eugene, *143*
Smith Michael, *16, 143*
Sorokin, Pitirím, 12, *18, 19, 143*
Sovani, N. J., *143*
Srinivas, M. N., 23, 24, 25, 28, *47, 48,* 49, *72, 143*
Stern, Claudio, *18, 143*
Stevenson, H. N. L., *143*
Stinchcombe, Arthur L., *18, 72, 143*
Stockman, Norman, *137*
Svalastoga, Karre, 14-15, *18,* 19, *144*

T

Thielbar, Gerald W., *144*
Treiman, Donald J., *17, 139*
Tumin, Melvin M., 8-9, 10, *18,* 19, *144*

V

Verba, Sidney, *144*
Vidyarthi, Lalita P., *144*

W

Wagatsuma, Hiroshi, *137*
Warner, W. Lloyd, *144*
Weber, Max, 6-7, 11, 22, *144*
Weiner, Myron, *144*
Wesolowski, Wlodzimierz, *18, 144*
Wiser, C. V., *144*
Wiser, W. H., *144*
Wrong, Dennis H., *18, 144*

Y

Yasuda, Saburo, *19, 144*